XFACTOR
UNMASKED

XFACTOR UNMASKED

THE RISE AND FALL OF ONE OF THE WORLD'S MOST KNOWN SUPERFANS

TY ROWTON

XFactor Unmasked
The Rise and Fall of One of the
World's Most Known Superfans
Ty Rowton

To contact the author:
kcxfactor7@gmail.com

Published by

Mary Ethel

Mary Ethel Eckard
Frisco, TX

Library of Congress Control Number: 2026910746
ISBN Print: 978-1-966561-45-3
ISBN eBook: 978-1-966561-46-0

All Scripture quotations, unless otherwise indicated, are taken from the Holy Bible English Standard Version (ESV), © 2001 by Crossway, a publishing ministry of Good News Publishers. ESV Text Edition 2025.

DEDICATION

This book is dedicated to everyone who has struggles, especially those who battle with addictions and mental illness.

The devil's number one way to attack is through our minds. He uses chemicals to destroy millions of lives; millions of others are attacked through mental illness. The only thing that works for me is to surrender it all to God. I also sprinkle in AA and NA, along with seeing a therapist to help in these areas. And I have an amazing circle from church, support groups, friends and family who encourage me to stay on the right path. I also take medications to help with my bi-polar, mania, depression and anxiety.

I've been beaten down and have lost everything, including hope. Those were scary times. God brought me through those storms and restored my hope. God has given me a foundation where I pray, and I help others by sharing how God has saved my life and is breaking the chains that once held me down. We all have things we struggle with and it's important that we help each other get through them. Everyone is unique and certain things work for us. Hopefully some of the things I've written about will help you.

I pray that you will gain hope through my testimony and that God will use this book to save just one life; if He saves more, then all glory and honor to Him. Prayer has been my greatest weapon to destroy everything the devil throws at me. And I pray for you, too, for whatever you are struggling with in your own life.

God bless you.

CONTENTS

FOREWORD

No one told me that the first time you look into your newborn's face, you experience instantaneous love. In our lives, love usually grows gradually, but when you become a mom, that love is there immediately.

Ty came into the world a happy baby who slept nine hours the first night at home and rarely had a bad day. While other babies had colic or were fussy, Ty stayed healthy and happy. He crawled, walked and talked early.

When Ty was 12 months old, I bought him a potty chair. He thought he was big stuff and carried it around with him that first day. Every time he used it, he cheered and clapped and, at the end of the day, he was potty trained! I didn't realize how unusual that was until I had my other boys and tried to potty train them!

Years ago, at a get together with friends and their babies and toddlers, a friend had been watching Ty and the other kids. She leaned over to me and said, "Anyone who has that good of a baby is going to have a mess when he grows up." Little did she know that she might have foretold what the future would hold with Ty.

Ty was born with dark brown hair, but it became bleached blond when he was old enough to go outside. That's because Ty loved all types of sports as a young boy and was either throwing and hitting a softball, a basketball, or later, a golf ball or bowling. He practiced constantly.

When he got a little older, along with a friend, they coached other little boys' teams. He's always been a people-person, had lots of friends, and never thought he was too good for anyone.

High school brought alcohol into his life and things began to change. Sports took a back seat to partying and he lost his drive to excel in sports. Looking back, college was just one big party for Ty. Not knowing how to help, we got him into treatment several times, but he always slipped back into the old ways. Addiction is a hard road to travel, both for the addicted and for all those who love them.

Once out of college, he began working at centers for the handicapped and thrived at helping other people. When I'd go visit him and we'd see his clients out in public, they'd run to greet him and give him a hug. One year, he took his one week vacation from work to drive an older client out of state to visit his 90 year old mother, as they hadn't seen each other for several years and she was about to die. His love for the handicapped wasn't fake; it was genuine. Little did we know that all his training would come into practice later in life when he received what he'd later say, the greatest gift of his life -his little girl.

I've always believed that God saved Ty for a purpose, and I've told him this throughout his life. He has survived numerous car wrecks and close calls throughout the years that probably should have killed him. Most people wouldn't have survived.

I received great joy and relief when I saw him accept Jesus and be baptized in Kansas City, even though his trials at that point were far from over. Still, I took it as a sign from God that he was on the right path.

A friend once told me, "Sometimes the worst thing that could happen turns out to be the best thing that can happen." I have definitely seen that play out many times since and most significantly in Ty's life. I was once told when Ty was in treatment to, "Let go and let God."

That's a tough thing to do when it's your child, no matter the age. But it's good advice, as God is the ultimate healer and redeemer.

Ty has seen the highest of highs and gotten to meet a lot of famous people, traveled extensively to games and events, and done some fun and amazing things in the last 30 years. But he's also trudged through the lowest of lows. He has survived and had to start over from scratch time after time, with not a dime in his pocket, and not remembering what the previous days or months held. We are not proud of some of the things he's done in the past with his addiction and later bi-polar, but we are most proud that he has never given up and has always picked himself up and kept fighting to survive and overcome his demons. Afterall, don't we all have our own demons? It's only by God's grace and salvation that we survive.

I now believe God saved Ty to help others who are struggling with addiction or mental illness, and I sincerely hope that Ty's story will help others. He knows that God's grace is what has saved him.

God Bless!
Deb Lawrence, Ty's Mom

INTRODUCTION

One choice can change the trajectory of an entire life. Little did I know that dressing up as a fan at Chiefs games would do that for me. The greatest blessing was how all my adventures, good and bad, led me to giving my life to God.

This is my journey from the lowest of lows to living in God's glory. Just like the song, God bless my broken road that led me to you.

At 4 a.m. one Sunday morning, I was headed toward the Arrowhead stadium for the biggest game of the year. That's when I got the call that one of my angels who had been battling cancer had gained her angel wings. I cried uncontrollably, as she had become an important part of my life.

As I rolled up to the parking lot at Arrowhead, many Chiefs fans surrounded my vehicle, asking for pictures. I said, "Please give me a couple of minutes to finish putting on my outfit." Honestly, I needed to compose my emotions. After a few minutes, I transformed from Ty to my alter ego, XFactor, which is always loud and proud.

I continued all day being a wild and crazy Superfan, working tirelessly to energize fans for this enormous game. 80,000 rabid fans distracted me from the phone call I had received at 4 a.m. At 6 p.m., I returned to my XFactor SUV after a day that will not be forgotten. Arrowhead was so loud, and enormous victory was accomplished. As I started to remove a few items of my outfit, the last fans approached for final pictures of the day. After talking for a while, I hopped into my SUV, which was about 70 degrees warmer than it had been outside the previous 13 hours.

Suddenly, my angel's death hit me hard. At this point in my life, I didn't have a strong relationship with God, so I turned to the tools I used to deal with pain. I cracked open my first beer and did a line of cocaine. I felt alone on the way home, as the fans who had mobbed me all day were going in different directions to their homes. I buried my pain in the bottom of a 30 pack of beer and in the bottom of my bag of cocaine. This was how I dealt with all of my emotions.

And this begins the journey of where my crazy adventures led me. Buckle your seat belt and enjoy the ride.

XFactor SUV

CHAPTER 1

Childhood

I grew up in Scott City, a small farming community in western Kansas. My mom and dad were divorced when I was 5 years old, which was hard on me throughout my youth. A couple of years later, my mom married an amazing man, so I grew up with two dads.

I was an adventurous kid, always taking on dares to do crazy stuff. At a young age, I fell in love with sports. I played every sport imaginable and watched ESPN religiously. I spent a lot of time playing by myself: basketball, football, throwing a baseball against the house, or playing golf. When I did this, I imagined I was playing against the heroes I watched on TV. I constantly dreamed of playing professionally and being famous.

I was a good athlete, but I was small. In my freshman year of high school, I was only 5'4" and weighed about 100 pounds, and I eventually gravitated toward partying, just like my dad. This is when I started living two different lives. My mom and stepdad were responsible and provided a stable, loving household, but they didn't approve of partying. On the other hand, my dad lived everyday like it was his last. He worked and played extremely hard, acting like my best friend. When I got in trouble with the law, he was who I called. He never punished me and he couldn't say too much because he had probably done much worse when he was my age.

When I was 7, I started working for my dad at his gas station. I also mowed yards or scooped snow in winter to make extra money. In high school, I worked on my granddad's farm during harvest and repairing elevators. I never dreamed of being a doctor, teacher, etc., like all the other kids. A career didn't excite me. I was always dreaming of being rich and famous. I knew early on that I didn't want to be like the rest of my family and live in my small town. I dreamed of the big city lights.

My early years sent me in directions that defined my life.

"At that time, the disciples came to Jesus, saying, 'Who is the greatest in the kingdom of heaven?' And calling to him a child, he put him in the midst of them and said, 'Truly, I say to you, unless you turn and become like children, you will never enter the kingdom of heaven.'"
Matthew 18:1-3

CHAPTER 2

Angels Appear in My Life

In 1994, my life was in a scary place. My peers in college introduced me to the world of drug dealing to support my habits. I knew that eventually only two things could happen: I would end up in prison or worse, dead.

It was scary having KBI watching my house, hearing stories of associates going to jail, seeing guns, and witnessing people getting beat up for screwing others over. Waking up every day in constant fear of what could happen was a horrible way to live. My roommate and I decided to quit selling drugs and get a real job.

We were hired at a facility that helps adults with disabilities learn independent skills. I went to work on the graveyard shift, 12 a.m. to 8 a.m. Instantly, the group home became a safe place from the crazy party world. I fell in love with individuals I helped, and they loved me as I brought humor into their lives. I made less money in a month than I did some days selling drugs, but I received something bigger than a paycheck; love from God's greatest gifts. They amazed me at how much happiness they got from the smallest things; for instance, a penny on the ground. I realized I was searching for happiness in complex things and struggled in that world. I thought their lives were boring and consistent, so why were they always so happy? Being addicted to thrills, adventures, and craziness, this way was different because they brought me peace.

This is when the roller coaster between God and the devil began. I did amazing things with His angels at work, but immediately rolled with the devil at home, throwing parties every day. I ate Romen noodles and bologna sandwiches because I didn't make much money, but I could justify spending more on alcohol than I did on food for two weeks. I started working lots of overtime, which was a blessing because I was sober at work, and the extra hours allowed me to be at my safe place.

I was promoted to house supervisor after 6 months. This was hilarious because outside of work I was a mess and never responsible. Eventually I was promoted to a new group called triage or emergency response team. I thrived in this role as I was paged when staff were having major problems with individuals who were violated. During my days selling drugs, I dealt with crazy situations where I had to resolve major issues; this job was like that. I was good at being a calming influence on individuals who were extremely upset. I excelled at conflict resolution between staff and individuals. Setting up activities that staff and individuals could do together really decreased behavior problems.

Three individuals we helped had a rare condition called Prader Willy. This condition caused them to always be hungry; they never felt the sensation of being full so they could literally suffocate themselves by eating too much. Also, they didn't metabolize food as fast, so they gained 8 times the weight as normal people. I worked hard with professionals to change their diets. We gave them a lot more food that was also healthier for them. This made them happy because it didn't seem like we were punishing them but rewarding them.

I also led by example in having fun places we could walk to. Staff were scared to take these individuals out in public due to fear they would become violent. The opposite happened as they loved being in public and meeting new people. I then helped them establish mowing businesses, which gave them self-worth and value. They loved making extra money so they could buy gifts for their girlfriends and families. It was an amazing activity the staff and they could do together. With increased exercise and a new diet, the pounds started flying off.

The next step was convincing management to allow them to have food locked up in their houses so we could teach them how to portion and how to cook. We did have issues with them tricking staff and getting more food; they were smart because their thoughts were constantly consumed by the urge to eat. I could relate because I always found ways to get alcohol and drugs, which was a constant craving. The key was that we worked together as a team to make it successful. By doing this, I was working myself out of a job, as fewer and less problem situations arose.

God then gave me new challenges as the government implemented a program called Community Inclusion. They wanted to transport people who had been institutionalized in state hospitals most of their lives into our organization. This was a huge learning curve, as I had to get to know individuals that mostly were nonverbal and who had major behavior issues they had learned from years of being institutionalized.

In state hospitals, funding was so limited that the ratio had been anywhere from 20-80 individuals per member of staff. This only allowed for basic needs to be met, never teaching them independent skills. They had learned that if they hit someone or did something bad, they would get attention from staff. All of a sudden, my task was to learn how to change years of learned behaviors so we could promote independence and protect my staff. This involved me basically living at their new house. We had to set up the environment and observe, taking notes all the time. Finding staff to work in these difficult environments was an enormous challenge as many quit after their first shift. It also strained my staff as we constantly asked them to work overtime.

During this time, I had been promoted to residential supervisor. I worked with three girls trying to fill shifts, as a lot of times we were 20 full-time employees short. I became manager over the men who had the worst behavior issues. I was constantly on call, and many times had to go to work where most staff wouldn't go. It was humbling and powerful to other staff because, yes, I was their boss, but I would also do the work I asked them to do. It also established trust that I was there for them no matter what the circumstance was. The individuals acted amazingly when I was around. They understood I was in an authority position but also was their friend and put their wants and needs first.

I got a call one night that changed my life. There was an emergency situation in a town 30 minutes away. Police had found an individual in a house where his caregiver mom was found dead. My boss said, "You are the best person we have; can you please go figure out the situation? I have very little information for you about this man."

Upon arriving, I talked to two police officers. They said there was no family to contact, and neighbors had only seen John out of the house a few times in his whole life. It broke my heart as he kept saying, "Momma." Later I figured out it was only a word that he knew. I investigated the situation and spoke words of comfort to him. I discovered that pillowcases were used as his adult briefs. I had no clue if he could use the restroom or feed himself, so I did the best I could. There was no TV in the house, so I found an old radio. I turned the radio on, and he began to scream and move his body. At first, I thought it scared him and he didn't want it on. I turned it off and he kept looking toward the radio saying, "Momma." I turned it back on and said, "Get, Get, Get Down, John!"

He immediately laughed at me. He had a bottle tied to his wheelchair that he began rattling. This was the moment our bond was formed. I spent the next three days getting to know John at his home till my organization could get the apartment ready for him. When I brought him to his new apartment, my boss said, "Go home and get some sleep." I answered, "I don't care if you pay me or not, I'm staying with him during this transition." I knew he was scared. The next few years, he would get so excited at the sound of my voice. A love and bond had been forever shaped. We were enormous XFactor's in each other's lives.

Recently, I found out John had grown his angel wings along with about 25 other individuals who were enormous XFactor's in each other's lives. I'm blessed they were in my life because they rescued me from a life where jail or death were my next steps. They were my angels.

Next, God placed me in my hometown after enormous personal storms ended my time in Great Bend. (I will tell you about that in the addiction chapter.) I moved back to my hometown and took a job at another facility. I was hired to fix problems at apartment complexes where they had enormous behavior issues. The manager, who had quit a few days before, had locked himself in the bathroom, and the individual broke down the door, threw the 300-pound manager out of the bathroom, ripped the toilet out of the floor, and threw it at the manager.

I knew I had a hard job ahead of me when I accepted this position. I used my experience to get to know my new individuals. I found out that staff did everything for them instead of teaching them, and they were too afraid to take them into the community. I discovered the main guy I was hired for had OCD, and if something was out of place or if change happened, he would become violent. He would give warnings saying, "That ain't right."

Studying him, I was able to structure his environment so that he didn't get frustrated. I discovered that he loved to clean and to cook; his house was important to him. I learned that he loved collecting pop cans and "get money" from them.

His dad wanted the staff to help him lose weight. So, I incorporated a healthier diet and every free minute I would take him places so he could walk and pick up pop cans. I also asked my friends to save cans for him. After working extremely hard in gaining his trust, he would say, "Ty said Yes" or "Ty said No" to staff. Then he would add, "He is the boss."

The lady who ran all of residential went on maternity leave and I was asked to run the residential program for 6 months. During this time, I instructed staff and individuals to call me with any problem. I could always find a solution over the phone or by coming on scene. One of my biggest struggles was communicating with some staff as they only spoke Spanish. I was blessed to have managers who could translate and teach staff a new way of doing things. Even though I was only there for two years, I left a footprint that lasted for years to come. These individuals were enormous XFactor's in my life as I really found creative ways to drastically improve their lives.

My next journey took me to Manhattan, Kansas. I took a residential staff position but, not being a manager, it didn't challenge me enough. Then I heard of a brand-new organization that was opening. I was interviewed and hired to help run residential. At first, I didn't like it because it was a faith-based-first organization. Drugs and alcohol had distanced me from God. I felt out of place with my parents as they were religious. I found that it was easy to connect with individuals, though, and immediately started implementing things I had learned over the years.

These individuals were highly functioning, so it was more challenging at first. I had the most amazing boss who thought outside the box, just like I did. Together we started implementing creative new things. My boss started putting me in charge of all day-to-day operations. I became manager over the day program, job service, residential, and staff training. We became involved with churches, rest homes, and many other volunteer charity organizations. We were able to get them to help the community, which allowed them to be loved and accepted by the community. We also grew by helping families learn about us and take an interest in getting their loved ones in our services.

One of the amazing things that happened: We had a mom who led our worship team where our individuals performed at local churches. This is where I first heard the song, "I can only imagine." That was the main song our individuals would sing and dance to in the churches we visited.

After 14 and half years of working 100 plus hours and always being on call, I walked away from being burnt out. God had started opening up charity opportunities with my involvement as XFactor. After leaving, I had many lifelong friends, both individuals and my staff. We stay in contact the best we can. Every time I pass through the cities where I worked, I make time to go see everyone. There is always instant love from individuals I worked for, and my love for them is forever! They impacted my life more than I ever did theirs. They were angels sent from heaven to help a wretch like me.

I was blessed to have helped around 100 individuals and countless thousands of staff. Getting to know so many amazing angels gives me courage to meet new angels. I confidently approach and talk to every angel I see, as they are God's greatest gifts to us. I thank God for the gift of love that fill them. I taught my staff to only see abilities, never disabilities.

I'm inspired by the angels on how they overcome things that we could never imagine and how they just love life, as simple as it may be. Step outside your comfort level and get to know them, I promise they will change your life just like they have mine. Out of everyone in the world, no one has been a greater XFactor to me than my angels!

"See, I am sending an angel ahead of you to guard you
along the way and to bring you to the place I have prepared."
Exodus 23:20

CHAPTER 3

Kyle

In 2000, my best friend asked me to move with him to Manhattan, Kansas. There was a month before I started my new job at a facility that helped individuals with special needs, so for 2 weeks, I did nothing but drink, which is how I dealt with change.

After drinking for 20 hours a day, I got extremely bored, so I searched for jobs in the newspaper. I came across a job for 4 hours a day helping a man with muscular dystrophy. I called and set up an interview with Kyle and his mom. I was immediately blown away by Kyle, who was the most kind, loving man. His condition left him with limited use of his arms and hands. His mom, who was in her late 70's, talked about previous caregivers who had stolen from Kyle, used him, and were not dependable in showing up for work, which meant she would have to take care of him. God placed on my heart to help them. The job only paid $10 an hour, and I would have to drive 15 minutes each way, four times a day. But this wasn't about the money; it was about becoming a stabilizing force in Kyle and his mom's lives.

After arriving the first morning, as soon as I opened his apartment door, I was greeted with a cheerful "Good morning, Ty, how are you?"

accompanied by the biggest smile. Kyle was patient and taught me what he needed. He quickly became a huge part of my life. He was positive, happy, caring, and loving, no matter what challenge he was facing.

I was a full blown alcoholic during this time, as I drank 7 days a week. Many trials came up due to my drinking, but Kyle was like my therapist. He was someone I could tell everything to, who didn't judge and who offered advice.

Kyle shared his life story with me. He lived a normal life until around age 25 when muscular dystrophy started. He walked, worked, and did everything we all take for granted. Never did he have sorrow for the way his life had turned. So many would be depressed and question, "Why me, God?" But Kyle counted his blessings and lived in them. He firmly lived in his abilities and never worried about his disabilities.

One day I asked Kyle if he wanted to join me and my friends at a bar. He had told me that one of his favorite things when he could walk was to shoot pool and drink a beer. That day he drove his wheelchair about a mile to meet us. After arriving, he asked my permission to have one beer, which cracked me up, as he was my boss and twice my age. His favorite was Bud Light, so I ordered him one. He said, "Please don't tell my mom." I laughed and said, "I would be in more trouble than you." I saw such joy as Kyle sipped on his beer and shot pool with us. It had been many years since he was one of the boys. My friends instantly fell in love with him. This became our once-a-week tradition. Kyle would tell the waitress no to a second beer saying, "I have to drive this wheelchair home, and I don't want to get a DUI." This cracked us up!

Kyle enjoyed living vicariously through me and the amazing things I experienced as XFactor. He taped every game and every news broadcast after the games, saving every clip that featured me on TV. One day I decided to buy him a football and get it autographed for his birthday. After the game that week, a bunch of players autographed the football, and I told them all about Kyle. After Lionel Dalton heard about Kyle, he jumped out of his car and retrieved a football from his trunk that had been autographed by the whole team. When I gave Kyle the two footballs, he smiled and said no one had ever given him such an amazing gift.

A couple of weeks later, there was a picture of me on the cover of the KC Star. I brought Kyle a copy that night and said, "Look, I've finally made it Big Time!" What he told me next forever changed my outlook on "fame." He said, "No Ty, you aren't on the cover of Manhattan Mercury. When that happens, you will have made it Big Time!" I laughed and said, "Only a few thousand would see that! Way more will see me on the cover of KC Star."

In Kyle's world, Manhattan Mercury was important. He literally lived next door to Mercury and read it every day. He had never read the KC Star. Later that evening, I went to get into my Chiefs XFactor car and there was a business card under the wiper from a reporter with the Manhattan Mercury asking me to call him. I called from Kyle's house, and he said he had seen a picture of me in KC Star and wanted to write about the famous XFactor living in Manhattan. I did an interview later that night.

The following Sunday, the reporter came to the bar to get pictures of me cheering during a Chiefs away game. He took a picture of Kyle and me screaming at the TV. The following Monday, a week after the KC Star cover picture, Kyle and I were on the front page of Mercury with a huge article about XFactor. Upon arriving at Kyle's apartment, he had the newspaper in front of him. He was beaming from ear to ear and said, "We have finally made it Big Time together!" It wasn't till later that it sank in. In Kyle's world, it wasn't about what I thought; it was about what he thought was Big Time. Even when I was inducted into the Pro Football Hall of Fame, Kyle didn't see that as big as being in Manhattan Mercury.

As time went on, I started helping Priest Holmes's "Team Priest." This pulled me to KC more often, away from Kyle. My friends who spent time with Kyle at the bar stepped up and cared for him when I was in KC. This was a blessing from God that took the burden from his mom, who wasn't physically capable of caring for Kyle.

Over the years, I saw Kyle's body slowly deteriorate. He became sick and had to be hospitalized. That's when they discovered his heart was failing, so they put a pacemaker in to keep him alive. For the next month, I would visit him every day at the hospital. One night, he told me he wanted so badly to go home. After many talks with his mom and doctors, we convinced them to discharge him. Kyle had life alert so he could call me anytime he needed me.

The night that he came home from the hospital, I told him I was going to stay all night and sleep in a chair. Kyle told me, "Go home. You have your other job, and I will call you if I need anything." I stayed much later than usual, talking to him. I cherished our talks. I didn't sleep well that night, waiting for a phone call from Kyle. The next morning, I awoke and had the sense that Kyle wasn't alright. I drove to his apartment and, for the first time in three years, I didn't hear, "Good morning, Ty, how are you?" I was gripped by fear as I knew what had happened. Walking into Kyle's room, he looked so peaceful, like he was asleep. I checked for a pulse, and his body was ice cold. I sat down and cried.

Being a CPR instructor, I knew it was too late to revive him, and Kyle had a DNR (Do Not Resuscitate). I called 911, which was the hardest call I've ever made. I called my boss at my main job, and he told me to take the time I needed. After hours with the police and paramedics, I called my friends who had helped with Kyle. We all took off work, went to the bar, drank, shot pool, and talked about Kyle. The next five days, I drank and cried. I had lost one of my best friends and didn't know how to deal with pain other than to drown it with alcohol.

At the funeral, I was the head pallbearer and the only one who had the strength to speak. I talked about Big Time, and I shared how Kyle was in Heaven, able to walk and do all the things he once could. I said Kyle has made it Big Time by being in Heaven.

Kyle taught me more than anyone. In the eyes of the world, he had very little, but in actuality, he had more than everyone else. He was my angel who taught me to live in my blessings and to love everyone no matter how they were created. Without God bringing Kyle into my life, I wouldn't be here to write this.

We all leave footprints on others we encounter. Physically, Kyle did something amazing that still impacts others. I had taken him to advocate meetings where he convinced city leaders to lower all buttons on every stop light so that kids and people in wheelchairs could reach them. That is his physical legacy. But more importantly, he was an enormous XFactor to everyone who was blessed to have him in their lives.

After Kyle's passing, God made it clear it was time to move to KC and on to the next chapter of my life. Kyle was the XFactor keeping me in Manhattan. When he left Earth, I was signaled to chase my dreams, knowing Kyle would forever be with me in my heart!

"The LORD has established His throne in heaven, and His kingdom rules over all. Praise the LORD, you His angels, you mighty ones who do His bidding, who obey His word. Praise the LORD, all His heavenly hosts, you His servants who do His will. Praise the LORD, all His works. Everywhere in His dominion. Praise the LORD, my soul."
Psalm 103:19-22

Jenna

God teaches us through our worst storms. After a storm destroys what once was, His blessings come when beautiful things grow from wreckage. This best explains circumstances with my daughter, Jenna, whose mom I met at a Chiefs Mitch Holthaus Show.

Here's the story. Jared Allen had been nominated as king in high school and college but hadn't won the crown, so he asked Chiefs Mitch Holthaus to find him a homecoming queen. Mitch asked me to dress up as a cheerleader to punk Jared, who was constantly playing jokes on us. I wore a Chiefs cheerleading outfit, a long blonde wig, red high heels, and had a weeks' worth of hair growth all over my body. I named myself Yolonda/Y-Factor from Sweden. Voting was done by applause, and when my name was called, the house erupted in cheers! I became Jared's first homecoming queen and danced with him for a couple of songs. After dancing with Jared, I was approached by a pretty girl who gave me her phone number and asked me to please call.

The next few months we started seeing each other, and she told me she was going through a divorce. I was dating other girls at the time, but slowly, I started spending more time with her. The first time my superfan buddy, Weirdwolf, met her, he nicknamed her "Saturday." He said, "I won't remember your first name because every time I see Ty, he has a different girl with him."

I always practiced safe sex because I feared STD's and having a child. I didn't want a kid to cause my so-called rock star lifestyle to disappear. But "Saturday" convinced me she was on the pill and protection wasn't necessary. Within a couple of months, she was pregnant. Then she told me she was still married and living with her husband, but he was addicted to porn, which was the reason she was always with me. She said now that she was pregnant, she was going to kick him out and wanted to just be with me. I started preparing myself to be a dad and embraced the news.

A month later she had a miscarriage. I loved her and wanted a family with her, so we started trying to get pregnant again. I was happy when the test came back positive a few months later. I was also introduced to her daughter from marriage and slowly started to adopt her as my daughter.

Two months into the pregnancy, everything changed. I got a call from "Saturday" screaming she had grabbed a broken lamp in her garage, which shocked her and threw her across the room. At the next doctor's appointment, we found out that there was very little water in the womb and she would have to go on bed rest.

All of a sudden, extreme jealousy started as she thought I would go running to other girls to escape the reality of having a child with a disability. God had prepared me for this challenge by putting me in a job where I was a manager for 14 years working with adults with disabilities. We went to a doctor's appointment to get an ultrasound of our child. Her arms were crossed making an X. I told the nurse, "I guess I won't need a DNA test." The nurse asked why? My girlfriend responded, "Don't get him started." I told the nurse I was XFactor and I make an X with my arms all the time. The nurse laughed and said, "This is definitely your daughter's XFactor."

As time went on, the news from the doctors got worse. The fluid levels kept decreasing with every visit. Our relationship began to suffer as "Saturday" blamed herself. Eight weeks before the due date, she was hospitalized and fluids were introduced intravenously. All of a sudden, the water level in the womb raised to normal levels. Why had the doctors not tried this earlier?

After a week in the hospital, the doctor said, "We are going to take this baby now." Seven weeks early. We were rushed into emergency C-section. The first time I saw my baby girl, my heart crashed. She was rolled into a ball that would easily fit in my hand. She was only 4 pounds, 1 ounce. With no water in the womb, she couldn't swim, so her arms and legs were locked against her little body. The doctors rushed her to ICU, so I couldn't be with my daughter on her first night on Earth.

I decided to leave the hospital and go to Jared Allen's Chiefs Show. I told Jared that I had named my daughter Jenna Allyn after him, since I met her mom the night that I was his homecoming queen. Her initials were JA and I changed the "e" to a "y" in Allen. Jared was so excited. Sadly, two months later, my good friend and godfather to my daughter was traded to the Vikings.

Jenna was transferred to Children's Mercy PICU unit for the next five weeks. It was tough not being able to hold my baby girl. On Jenna's first night out of the hospital, we took her to the Mitch Holthaus Show. Carl Peterson, Mitch, Herm Edwards and QB Brodie Croyle held her more than I did. How many kids have been held by celebrities?

My mom told me when Jenna was born that God sent her to me because I was the perfect dad to handle her challenges. She also said that God sent her to me to save my life. This opened my eyes to the truth as I had struggled with addictions for many years.

Having a baby girl changed my life. Never had I loved someone so much. As she grew, she loved everything Daddy loved, especially going to charity events; anything involving the Chiefs, bowling, fishing, etc. Her favorite player became Jamaal Charles, which blew me away, because he had learning disabilities while he was growing up. Jamaal was in special education classes and had risen above it all to become a superstar running back. It was like Jenna could sense this, and I believe that is why she fell in love with him. She would tell everyone that Jamaal Charles was her favorite player because he held her when she was a baby. She was exactly the same way to kids with disabilities where she instantly connected with all of them.

Early in life, Jenna was afraid of the KC Wolf and would cry every time he came near. But one day, KC Wolf grabbed her baby doll and rocked it. Jenna laughed and instantly fell in love with him. When KC Wolf fell and almost died, Jenna constantly asked, "Is he going to be alright, Daddy?" When KC Wolf's book came out, she wanted to go see him and get his book. It became her favorite book, and his story of how he overcame so many injuries inspired her.

One day I asked Jenna what her favorite color was. She answered, "Yellow, Daddy, because you already claimed red." That day I nicknamed her Y-Factor. Jenna's favorite thing to do became going to charity events so she could meet other angels. One year she asked if we could take other angels to preseason games with us. The first year we took five kids and their families. I had my friends throw a huge tailgate party for them. I had always thought preseason games were boring compared to regular season games. That changed when I saw kids with cancer and disabilities having the time of their lives. The cancer and disabilities disappeared, and they were just normal kids sharing something amazing together.

When we said our goodbyes, the parents cried as they explained how much their families needed this day. I cried happy tears, too, knowing this had forever changed my life. Angels had brought complete strangers together and instantly brought us all together as family. Being a dad whose daughter had many operations and spending so much time in the hospital, I could cherish what other families were going through.

The next summer, Jenna was getting ready to have double hip replacement surgery, where they were going to break her hips and put plates in so her legs would be straightened out in front of her. Early in the morning while sitting in the waiting room with my daughter, my phone was constantly going off. Loved ones were asking what gifts Jenna wanted. When I asked Jenna, without hesitation, she said, "Daddy, tell everyone to buy Chiefs tickets and parking so we can take even more angels to preseason games this year."

My eyes filled with tears. That was one of the sweetest things a dad could hear. Most kids would be selfish, wanting this and that. My amazing daughter, on one of the scariest days of her life, was thinking about other's needs and not her own.

Jenna's condition is rare and called Arthrogryposis. It's where tendons and ligaments don't develop correctly due to lack of water in the womb. It affects everyone differently, but Jenna has the most severe form of Arthrogryposis which affects her arms, legs and hips. She has limited use of her legs, but she can raise them a few inches. At a young age, from a seated position, she taught herself how to raise one leg at a time and wiggle her body so she could scoot across the floor. I encouraged her to walk everywhere in the house instead of carrying her. Also, her hands, fingers and arms have no movement. She learned to swing her arms with the rest of her body and drag where she could grasp things. She also taught herself how to use her mouth as her hands.

At a young age, she started drawing, coloring and writing by using only her mouth. On phone and tablet, she learned how to use her nose to scroll and then click on things she wanted to watch. Being a dad who promotes independence, I thought I was good at doing this. Jenna taught me to completely remove myself from everything, that I didn't need to teach her how to do things, she figures them out best on her own. Once in a while, she can't do something and we will find a creative way to make it happen.

When I bought her a camera, it was the best demonstration of her abilities. She was only 5 years old and had been begging me to buy her a camera so she could take pictures at charity events. At first, I thought this was going to be way too much for her, but I bought her a nice camera that was extremely slim and small. We went to a charity event where I was going to be bowling with Chiefs players and other celebrities. I went to help Jenna take pictures and she said, "Daddy, I can do it by myself." I was amazed as she grabbed the strap with her teeth, positioned the camera on her arm, then hit the power button with her nose. She told cheerleaders, "Say Chiefs," and she used her nose to hit the button to take pictures.

Later that night, she wanted to download pictures onto the computer so we could look at them. It was amazing all 780 pictures turned out from the event. I couldn't take better pictures than my daughter and I have full use of all parts of my body. Jenna taught me that I was actually holding her back by trying to help her. She grew up helping Daddy cook, clean, or whatever I needed to work on. Just like Kyle taught me about being one of the boys, my daughter taught me she loved helping, which is one of her purposes.

Jenna and Me at Chiefs Training Camp

One day a kid asked Jenna why her arms and legs were the way they were. She simply said, "It's because God made me this way." I had always battled with anger from the way people stared at and avoided angels I had taken into the community. With one short sentence, Jenna took all that away. It made me realize that God makes us all different and gives us each the ability to impact others.

My daughter has grown into the most amazing artist, winning talent shows and inspiring everyone who meets her. It's inspirational to others to see that she can do most things that we take for granted with the limitations she has physically. So many people say, "I'm so sorry" when they first see her. I always answer, "Please don't say that.

I wouldn't change anything about her. God made her a living angel." After a few minutes of observing Jenna, they always say, "Wow, she is beyond amazing."

Jenna and other angels have taught me to only live in their abilities and never to focus on their disabilities. We all have disabilities that aren't visible, one of the greatest ones is that we can't do something. These amazing kids teach us that anything can be accomplished if we try hard enough, and there are many different ways to accomplish our goals. These kids don't know they aren't supposed to be able to do something, they just go for it!

Jenna has been the greatest XFactor in my life. She has taught me more about life than school ever could. Many say I inspire them but, honestly, my angels have inspired me way more than I could ever inspire anyone else. I thank God daily for bringing Jenna into my life, as I'm blessed with the sweetest, most loving and caring person I've ever met. She brought a whole new meaning to loving someone unconditionally.

Jenna saved my life. I have chosen to quit drugs and alcohol because she deserves a sober dad and one that isn't going to die at a young age. Even though my relationship with her mom has been the worst storm of my life, I wouldn't change it for the world because God has given me the greatest gift in Jenna. All the blessings she brings far outweigh the storms that have occurred. I know that Jenna will take over things I've accomplished in the charity world and take it to a level I can't even imagine. As Daddy, I will always be her XFactor and she is forever my Y-Factor!

> *"As a father has compassion on his children, so the*
> *Lord has compassion on those who fear him."*
> Psalm 103:13

CHAPTER 4

Shon and Grace

Through charity work, I met an angel who impacted my life beyond words. Shon was paralyzed due to a wreck he was in when he was five years old. The paralysis also challenged his speech. While in the hospital, he flat lined for the first time. Instantly Shon and I became best friends. Our sense of humor was so similar. Shon was able to say few words verbally, but he had been taught sign language by his granddad that only the family completely understood. His family had to interpret what he was saying to me, but Shon's nonverbal's were spot on. Every time we were together, we would teach each other. Shon would roll his eyes, shake his head, and then look to God at my off-the-wall words. I would tell Shon, "God can't save you from me, you are stuck with me."

Shon loved the Chiefs as much as I did. I started taking him to Chiefs draft parties, to training camp, and to preseason games. He also loved going to charity events with me. Over the years, an amazing bond formed as did our love for one another. He also loved pretty girls and was always trying to touch their butts. I would say, "Behave, you are going to get slapped!" But of course, no girl would ever slap him. The first time I introduced him to the Chiefs cheerleaders, I said, "Shon you can't grab their butts because they are professionals." Shon's face turned bright red, and a huge smile spread across his face. All through picture taking, I would say, "Shon, you behave."

Our relationship grew when I started going to church with him. Shon wanted to stand and walk with assistance. During church I would support him standing while we sang. Then I would help him walk to the front during the altar call. God was an enormous part of Shon's life. He would sign about how he had died five times and how God had sent him back. Yes, Shon had seen the light five times and in his limited communication could tell us about it. He was a medical miracle, defying all odds since his wreck. The day I got baptized, Shon wanted to also be baptized. When it came Shon's turn, I helped him walk to the tank, then picked him up and carried him into the water. Going through his baptism was beyond powerful. I knew Shon was one of God's angels He had used to change my life.

The next year I got news that Shon was in the hospital, and chances were slim that he would make it. I called Derrion, the oldest son of Derrick Thomas, to go see him. For years, Derrion has gone to hospitals to visit angels, doing what his dad had done. At the hospital, Shon was so weak. I thought this was the last time I would see him alive. I gave him a Chiefs shirt I had made. Derrion and I autographed it for him. Shon always wanted all my Chiefs stuff. I had given him a bandanna, sunglasses, and necklaces like I wear as XFactor. Shon battled like a champ and shortly after we visited, he made a full recovery. Through Shon's challenges, I knew God kept pulling him through to inspire others. I was one that he always inspired in everything he did. He never complained but always tried to do things we take for granted.

A few months later, I got a call that floored me. It was from Shon's uncle; he had suddenly passed away. I jumped into my car to drive to Missouri City where he lived. God had the wheel of my car because I was crying and couldn't see. Upon arriving, I got out of the car as the hearse with Shon's body passed by. His mom was crying. I gave her a hug, and she said, "Son, I can't let him go; this isn't happening." The family had adopted me and always called me their son. I said, "Mom, Shon's body is here, but God has called his spirit home. He isn't with us anymore." I then said, "Now he will be with us always. He is an angel that has grown his angel wings." That night God placed words in my mouth to comfort everyone who gathered, which I had previously struggled to do.

The family asked me to help pay for the funeral expenses, as they didn't have much money. For the next week, I auctioned off many of my treasured memorabilia to raise money. Shon died on a Sunday evening, and the family told me how, that morning in church, Shon had spent all service signing and looking toward God. He had never done this continually in church. I believe God had started the process of calling him home, and Shon knew it was about to happen.

That Wednesday, we had planned to take Shon to the Chiefs Training Camp to get his brand-new Chiefs wheelchair autographed. I convinced his mom that we still needed to go. I asked some of my buddies to help. The first autograph was from Shawn Barber, former Chiefs linebacker. What a God thing: same names.

We then found some cheerleaders and I bought Shon a cheerleading calendar, just like I had done many times before. While telling cheerleaders about Shon, I pulled up his picture. Tears filled the head cheerleaders' eyes and she said, "Oh my. Shon is the one that is always with you, XFactor." She had been taking pictures with him for the previous seven years. Each time Shon had been with her, for just a few minutes each time, he had touched her heart (and not her butt).

The next Monday, I went to Missouri City at 5 a.m. to help the family. I was able to give them the money I had raised and donations out of my savings. This brought ease to the family. I had been asked to be a head pallbearer for Shon. On my way to the funeral, God placed on my heart to give Shon my red hair that I wore as XFactor; he had asked for it many times before, but that was the only wig I had, so I just laughed and said, "No." Now, just two days before, at a preseason game, my angels had decorated it with yellow beads and given it back to me.

At the funeral, his aunt began singing *Amazing Grace*. I cried and fell to my knees at the head of Shon's casket. I had been so strong for the family, but I hadn't been for myself. The family got on the floor with me and comforted me.

At the end of the service, the family wanted me to autograph his casket and then have everyone else in attendance sign it too. Shon loved autographs and now he would have all his loved ones with him. As people came forward, I constantly looked at Shon, wearing the shirt I had made him, my sunglasses and bandanna. Also in the casket was the autographed Chiefs cheerleading calendar. He was wearing my red dreads, which looked amazing on him. The wig was going with my angel to Heaven and had been adorned by angels still living on earth. Carrying Shon's body to his final resting place was emotional, but I had done this many times with loved ones. I thought about everyone else I had carried to their final resting place.

Following the funeral, my body started crashing. I had spent the last eight days going nonstop trying to balance work, Chiefs, and Shon's funeral. Driving home, I felt like I was going to fall asleep behind the wheel. After getting home, I slept six hours and woke up to a message from a Facebook friend I hadn't met. He told me he had an angel who loved seeing videos of me and asked if I could send her an autographed XFactor picture. I asked, "Where is your angel? I would love to meet her and bring her some gifts." He answered, "Eudora." This was close to where I was going to meet some friends, so I grabbed a couple of angel gift bags and drove the 45 minutes listening to *Amazing Grace* and *Angels Among Us*.

I had the address, but I just followed signs that God placed on the roads, so no navigation. I was traveling down an old highway when I came up behind red and yellow flashing lights on the back of a tractor. I slowed down and that's when I saw signs of a tornado that had come through months ago. I thought about my life and how it had been like a tornado destroying it. I saw rebuilding and growth happening where total destruction had recently been. I felt the exact same thing was happening in my life. The tractor then turned down an old back road, and I decided to follow it, just like I did as a kid following my granddad in his tractor. He pulled into a farm where the tornado had hit. He had been out growing crops even though his farm still had so much devastation.

I followed this road for a few miles, and it ended up in Eudora. I stopped at a convenience store and a man said, "You should go see James's angel. She is huge Chiefs fan, and he works here." I asked, "Where do they live?" and he said, "Just two blocks away." There was a row of trailers, and I stopped at trailer 5 because it had Chiefs flags. I knocked on the door and asked for James. The girl who answered said, "That's my brother, he lives in trailer 8." That really hit me as Derrick Thomas was my favorite player and wore number 58; that is also my birthday: 5-8. Another sign from God was James' address. He lived at 1200 Church Street. 12 is the number that is always on my Chiefs jerseys representing the fans / 12th man.

When I knocked on the door, James opened it and said, "This is my daughter, Grace." I about hit the floor because I didn't know her name yet. *Amazing Grace* had been playing constantly on my Pandora since Shon's aunt had sung it twice at his funeral. I said, "Hi, Amazing Grace." James said, "That's what we call her."

Grace came and hugged me like she had known me forever. All of a sudden, my phone rang with a tomahawk chip ring tone and Grace started doing the chop, pointing at my phone, so I gave it to her. I was getting introduced to the whole family when I heard *Amazing Grace* playing. I sat down with Grace and looked at my phone; she had clicked on YouTube and started playing that song. I remember thinking, "Wow, God is showing me so many signs." Little did I know what was about to happen.

Grace sat on my lap as I began taking all her gifts out. She was so excited and started taking the gifts to her mom. I thought both bags were completely empty, but I reached into the last bag to double check. My whole body started shaking as I felt the last thing in the bag. My arm was trembling as I pulled it out. I then saw my red dreads that I had buried Shon in only eight hours earlier. Somehow the hair that was in a grave in Missouri City, MO was now in Eudora, KS over an hour away. This scared me more than anything ever had. Here was God showing me He was real. From Shon's leaving, He had replaced him with His Grace. I was so shaken that I told the family I had to go as I had much to do.

In all honesty, I was too scared to stay there anymore. I started driving away and felt the feeling and movement of my body leave me. It felt like I was being paralyzed, unable to control my vehicle, but thank God my foot had fallen off the gas petal. In slow motion, I ran into a pedestrian sign. This was when God took over my body and I felt like a puppet. Eventually he pointed my head at a porch light. As I stared at it, the prettiest lights imaginable appeared. A purple, yellow and then red light expanded brightly around the white light. An image started emerging. It looked like the face of Jesus or our Father in Heaven, I'm not quite sure which it was.

As soon as I saw God's face, I got movement back into my body. I thought I had died in the crash and now was going to Heaven. But looking at the wreck, I thought, "I can't be dead from that," so I was confused about what was happening. I was too scared to drive anymore, and my phone was dead. So, I decided to walk back to James's house.

Before I made it back, two police officers stopped me and put me in handcuffs; they then took me back to the accident scene, performed a sobriety check, thinking I was drunk. After all, no sober person wrecks in a residential area. They were amazed when I was finished. They said no one had done all the tests so well. I felt numb and God had all five of my senses working like they never had before. It felt like I had super-powers. I didn't know how to handle what had just happened, so I fell into spiritual warfare which is described later in this book.

This is how God's grace entered my life. I found out later that Grace is related to Shon. Grace is so much like Shon in that he could only say a few words and uses sign language. She also shakes her head at me when I do or say something silly.

Through Grace, I completely and fully believe in God. Through Shon, I got to see God in the light just like he had many times. Just like God had sent Shon back five times because his purpose wasn't yet fulfilled, I've been given the same opportunity; a second chance. I just needed these things to happen to open my eyes and understand that God is real.

"Yet God, in his grace, freely makes us right in his sight.
He did this through Christ Jesus when he freed
us from the penalty for our sins."
Romans 3:24

"God saved you by his grace when you believed.
And you can't take credit for this; it is a gift from God.
Salvation is not a reward for the good things we have done,
so none of us can boast about it."
Ephesians 2:8-9

"But he gives more grace.
Therefore it says, 'God opposes the proud
but gives grace to the humble.'"
James 4:6

CHAPTER 6

Angels Amongst Us

God has blessed me by putting more angels in my life than I could count. The ones who battle cancer, major illnesses, and disabilities are the ones who have touched my heart the most. Here are six who are God's greatest gifts sent to forever change our lives.

Dawson

A family I was close to at Arrowhead invited me to visit their family member, Dawson. His twin brother, Christian, had the same challenges. The twins were born premature and both were in wheelchairs for their entire lives. I took Derrion, DT's son, with me to visit Dawson at the hospital. Dawson could not take his eyes off of me. When I wasn't in sight, he tracked my voice. His grandmother said he was smiling the entire time I was in the room.

A couple of days later, Dawson gained his angel wings. Even though my time with Dawson was short, he impacted my life. He was the first angel I visited at the hospital to grow his angel wings. He lit a fire in me to visit more angels because I could bring happiness into their lives and they would forever become a part of my heart.

I had a phobia of going to hospitals, as I didn't want to experience the pain of losing loved ones. Dawson changed this in me. My mom's song for me has been Leeann Womack's *"I Hope You Dance."* Just like that song, I decided to be a part of sick angel's lives, to not sit it out but to dance with them. Knowing how much pain could happen if they passed away, the blessings would outweigh that pain. Dawson taught me that even when facing death, we can have nothing but joy filling our hearts.

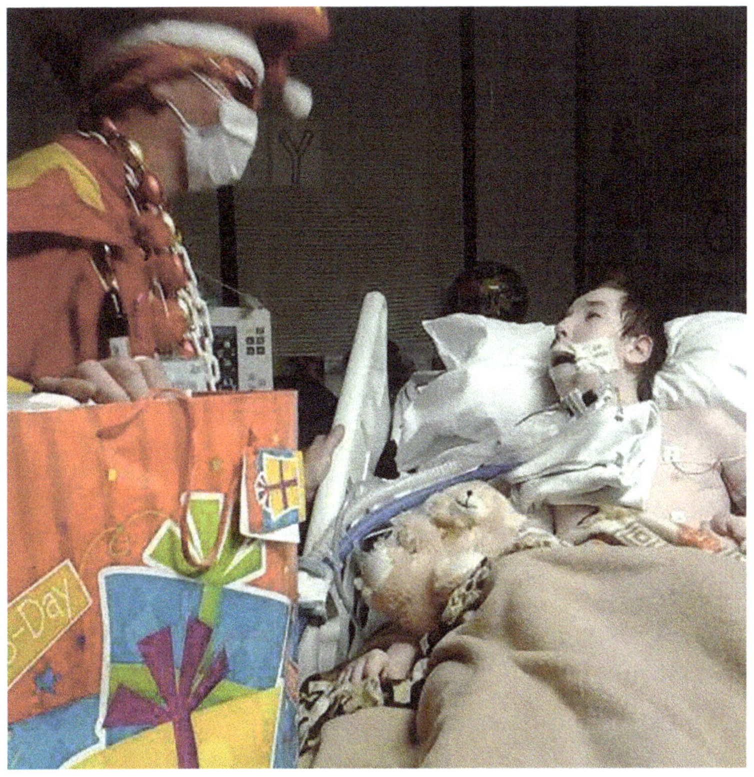

Visiting angel Dawson in the hospital. He gained his angel wings a couple of days later

Chris

Shortly after Dawson's passing, I was invited to visit an angel named Chris who was an enormous Chiefs fan. At the hospital, I met his dad, Butch, who happened to be a huge Bronco's fan.

Chris was in the hospital after having surgery to remove a brain tumor. Chris and I bonded instantly, as we both had the same ornery personality. Chris called me Mario, which his dad would say, "No, this is XFactor, the guy we always see on TV." Finally, after calling me Mario about 10 times, Chris made a motion like playing Nintendo. Maybe the drugs the doctors had him on made me look like Super Mario to him. I was flattered as this was my favorite game as a kid.

After Chris got out of the hospital, we became close, spending a lot of time together. We gave everyone a hard time and teased them. I was honored to help Chris stand in his father's wedding and to sign the marriage certificate. Chris was unstable on his feet due to cancer. We both were decked out in our Chiefs garb. His dad and new mom were decked out in their Broncos gear. This would be the last time for me to see Chris alive.

He taught me so much about how laughter and love were the best way to battle cancer. I never heard him feel sorry for the hand dealt to him. Chris made me laugh more than anyone in my life. Cancer never even came close to consuming him; instead, he consumed life! I now use what Chris taught me: when the devil attacks, simply laugh at him and do not allow him to steal my joy.

Caden

During the same time, I met an angel named Caden who was battling cancer. He wanted to be a police officer when he grew up, so a group of police officers adopted him as a junior deputy. Caden had beaten cancer just a year before, but it had returned to a different location. I was invited to go with the officers to the hospital, and we accompanied Caden to his first chemo treatment appointment.

During his chemo treatments, I became good friends with Caden. He enjoyed going to Chiefs events. My daughter Jenna and Caden became friends and enjoyed doing things together. They bonded and could relate to what each other were battling. We threw the biggest party for Caden when we got news that God had healed his cancer for the second time!

A year later, the cancer had returned for a third time. This time, though, it had spread to his spine and brain, so it was terminal. Caden battled like a champion, even though it would take a miracle. I watched his body as cancer deteriorated it. At his birthday party, I knew time was drawing near when he wouldn't be with us anymore.

The decision was made to put him in hospice so he could be comfortable in his home. Every night I joined the police officers going to his house to see him and talk to him. I learned from my grandpa that even though Caden was unconscious, he could still hear us. Caden loved being a prankster and joking so I tried bringing laughter and happiness to him. I told him how much I loved him and that I would teach other angels battling cancer what he had taught me: How to live life to the fullest, doing all the things they loved and to laugh always.

I was at the house the morning Caden grew his angel wings. Through all highs and lows of battling cancer twice, our love for each other was constant. I gained inspiration from Caden by the way he battled like a warrior. His life was short on earth, but he touched the souls of so many people who loved him with all their hearts.

Justice

When I met Caden, I was introduced to an angel also battling cancer named Justice who was full of life and loved to dance. Justice was going through chemo for the first time when our lives came together. My first hospital visits to see her, I told her I needed an older angel like her to help me with all my younger angels. She was excited about helping others, as she had the biggest heart.

This became her motivation during rough times. Her mom would say, "You need to battle through this, so you can get better and help XFactor's other angels." Justice amazed me; even though I knew she didn't feel well, nothing stopped her from being at every charity where I went to help. The joy this gave her melted my heart. I knew it was her purpose and also her motivation to beat cancer.

Justice and my daughter became best friends. They wanted to spend as much time together as possible. Their challenges made them closer because other kids couldn't relate to what they were battling. The girls loved dancing together and wanted to teach me the newest dance moves. Of course, I can't dance and did wrong moves, which would bring laughter to them.

Justice beat cancer only to have it return a few months later. I would go visit her often and help other angels, especially at Chiefs preseason games, had lit a fire in her to beat it once again. After another round of chemo, she once again got news that it had left her body again. A few months later we got news that cancer had returned for the third time. This was extremely scary, as Caden had just lost his battle the third time.

I saw on social media that Justice losing her beautiful hair was extremely upsetting to her. I went to the hospital with Big Cat Royals Superfan with a pair of clippers. I asked her to shave our hair so we could be beautiful to her. This really brought her a lot of laughter and happiness. Justice thought it was hilarious seeing me bald.

Later that week, I challenged all my Superfan buddies across America to find angels battling cancer and let them shave them also. It was amazing to see how many men answered this challenge. I got to see famous men I know, worldwide, being humble and selfless. They were making angels feel special and normal at same time.

On one visit to see Justice, her throat was hurting from chemo. She had to swallow a dye so they could run tests. I told Justice to make me the nastiest drink she could imagine. So, she had nurses get the craziest combination of ingredients which they blended together. I would take a drink of this nasty concoction and make a bitter beer face. She would laugh at my silly faces and then we would encourage her to have a drink. As teammates, we challenged each other and made it through our drinks together. When Justice got news that she had beat cancer for a third time, a huge relief came over me.

This was the feel-good story in the middle of our 2 angels who had grown their angel wings. Justice continues to be involved with charity activities and is an enormous inspiration to angels battling challenges that she conquered. It's so fun watching Justice grow from a kid to an amazing young women. She recently graduated high school, and her story impacts more lives than I can imagine.

Aimee

Through Justice, I met an 8-year-old angel named Aimee. She was battling cancer for the third time in her short life. Immediately, Aimee wrapped me around her finger and touched my heart. She was the sweetest, most caring little girl I had ever met.

When she was well enough, we took her to a draft party at Arrowhead. Aimee had the time of her life doing such an amazing event with kids who were similar to her. A few months later, I got to spend time with her at a Royal's game. The Royals had made a special night for her where she got to meet most of the players before the game and she got an autographed glove, bat, and ball from the team. Aimee was able to help Justice and me at a few charity events, which brought her excitement.

At 12:04 on May 8, 2017, I got a call that devastated me. Aimee had grown her angel wings. I had just turned 42 only four minutes earlier and went from happy to grieving. The story of how I handled her passing is in another chapter but let me just say it rocked me at my core.

Aimee's legacy lives strong today. Her parents and family have a charity event in her honor to raise money for cancer research. I've been blessed to make appearances as XFactor and have been able to see all the lives she impacted in her short 8 years on Earth.

Aimee inspires me to help more kids who battle cancer. It was precious watching as she cared for others first, even though it was her that was facing death. She was an angel in every sense of the word, filled with peace, unconditional love for everyone, and joy that was contagious.

Brianna

Many years ago, I met the most adorable angel named Brianna or Bri. She was the sweetest little girl who battled many challenges. Every time I saw her, she would give me hugs and kisses. One year she asked me to be her date for the Special Olympics dance. We had an unbelievable night dancing together. Brianna introduced me to every one of her special friends. During one dance, the lead singer put the microphone in front of her. Bri grabbed the mic and began singing. She was a superstar like that, never scared to try anything.

Her uncle called me one night, out of the blue, to let me know that she had grown her angel wings while she was sleeping. At her funeral, I met many new angels. It was apparent that everyone loved her as much as I did. She will forever be the prettiest date I've taken to a dance and, by far, the most entertaining one. Her legacy was to live to the fullest, doing absolutely everything she wanted to do, and she was full of more love than 100 others.

All my angels, whether on Earth or in Heaven, have taught me more about life than anyone. How they deal with pain and death helps me do the same. They each have amazing gifts to laugh, love, and wrap everyone around their fingers. Never do you hear negative things from them, but they stay in the positive things in their lives. When I battle enormous challenges, I ask myself, "How would my angels handle this?" If I follow that answer, then the solution is easy.

These are angels / God's greatest gifts because He makes them perfect inside. So many only see outside imperfections, but if you give them a chance, they will change your life. They will soften your heart and inspire you more than anyone ever will.

I'm beyond grateful to have amazing experiences and memories with these kids. So many people praise me for helping them, but the truth is, they help me a million times more than I help them. These angels are by far the biggest XFactor on Earth for me!

"Do not forget to show hospitality to strangers, for by so doing some people have shown hospitality to angels without knowing it."
Hebrews 13:2

"Then I looked and heard the voice of many angels, numbering thousands upon thousands, and ten thousand times ten thousand. They encircled the throne and the living creatures and the elders. In a loud voice they sang: 'Worthy is the Lamb, who was slain, to receive power and wealth and wisdom and strength and honor and glory and praise."
Revelation 5:11-12

CHAPTER 7

My Son, Alvin

In college, I lived my life as the ultimate party boy. My house was where everyone came to let their hair down and where anything was allowed. This lifestyle brought many girls into my life.

I had a short relationship with a girl who had been dating my roommate off and on. A few months later, word came through the grapevine that she was pregnant. At first everyone thought it was my roommate, as he had been with her the previous six months. We learned that she was moving to California and giving the baby up for adoption. Fast forward 17 years. I posted Happy Birthday to a girl I had dated back in my college days. She saw my post and told her husband, "That's our son's biological father." A couple of days later, I received an email from her husband saying, "I have raised your boy the last 17 years. This isn't about money. I just want my son to know his biological father." I had wondered if this baby was mine. Did I have a son out there? I was surprised that she never gave him up for adoption.

I called the father and expressed my concern that I believed my roommate was the father and not me. He suggested that we meet in Kansas City and do a DNA test. But even before the DNA test, I saw Alvin and knew he was my son. He had many of my physical traits. Five days later, the results came back, and Alvin was indeed my son. You hear stories like this, but it rocks your world when it happens.

My son entered my life when I was consumed in partying. I was a horrible role model. Spending time together, he was forced to protect me and make sure I didn't get into trouble. Alcoholism had completely consumed my life, which was a complete disaster. We did some amazing things together, such as Chiefs Training Camp and a few Chiefs game. This meant the world to me, as this is what I had done with my father. Alvin was at my house in 2012 when an intervention was done by my family and when I decided to go to treatment. Over the years, our relationship hasn't been as close as I wish it would be. This is my fault as it got off to a rocky start due to my addiction problems. Alvin is like I was in my younger years, in his 20's and experiencing the world. Just like me, Alvin has experienced many challenges; I guess it's in our DNA to live a crazy lifestyle.

Alvin has an amazing heart and would do anything to help others, but just like me, partying gets in the way of finding our purpose through God. I pray that he won't have to struggle like I did for most of my life. I learned, though, I had to go through my trials to get where I am today. Those struggles where I learned are teaching moments. When I decided to walk away from XFactor, I thought Alvin might fill my shoes. But God has a different purpose for him which is not to follow in my footsteps but to create his own path.

I always wanted a boy. As a matter of fact, when I found out I was going to be a dad, I prayed that Jenna would be a boy. Thank goodness God didn't answer that prayer, as Jenna is the light of my world. Who would have guessed that prayer for a boy had been answered 17 years prior. I know in my heart that Alvin will impact the world in an amazing way. So much love fills my heart for my son. God will be glorified in the end when amends are made on my part, and when Alvin gets a father role model he so deserves.

*"Hear, my son, your father's instruction, and
forsake not your mother's teaching."*
2 Corinthians 6:18

*"And I will be a father to you, and you shall be sons
and daughters to me, says the Lord Almighty."*
Proverbs 1:8

CHAPTER 8

My Mom, My Dad, and My Stepdad

Mom

I was my mom's first child, born on Mother's Day after 22 hours of labor. This was a sign of how hard a struggle I would be in future.

My mom and my dad divorced when I was 5 years old. Mom started a babysitting business so she could be with me at all times. Growing up was fun as I always had friends at our house. She was involved in every aspect of my childhood, and she was at every function and game, cheering me on.

A few years after the divorce, she married an amazing man. In my teenage years, I rebelled against them as they were my disciplinary parents. My mom neither drank nor did drugs. When I started partying and getting into trouble with the law, it put a strain on our relationship. She loved me and wanted the best for me and tried to protect me from the world, so she bailed me out of trouble. Looking back, I should have listened to her advice, but I had to learn on my own.

My mom is one of the most caring, loving, giving, hardworking, humble people I know. Her traits that I inherited would eventually help me cast out my own demons. God is an enormous part of my mom's life. She is successful because she glorifies Him. All through my life's struggles, one thing was constant; my mom was praying for me.

In 2012, after going to addiction treatment, our strained relationship began to heal. She had watched me killing myself with drugs and alcohol. In treatment I learned that my addiction was hurting her more than it was hurting me. It was causing her pain, constantly worrying and wondering if I was going to die. I learned that she stayed up at night, horrified the phone would ring with news that I was no longer alive.

When my daughter was born, I saw Mom's love blossom. My daughter brings her happiness without all the stress I bring. When I relapsed in 2017, it was my mom who came to rescue her son, again. Even through times when I had given up on myself, she never gave up. Since I was a kid, my mom would plant seeds in my heart about God. Finally, these seeds started to grow, and that's when true healing happened in our relationship.

For most of my life, I would lie to her about what was happening so she wouldn't be hurt and constantly worrying. By inviting God into my life, I no longer had to hold anything from her. When I was saved and baptized, my mom was in attendance, which was the best gift I could give her. She had always been my rock and my foundation, but when I made God my rock and foundation, so much more healing came.

By turning my life over to God, I've realized all the things my mom did to make sure I wouldn't completely sink. God is her foundation in everything she does. She puts God first in every aspect of her life. She is my hero, best friend, and someone I strive to be like. Her love for others is unmatched. She is always a positive X Factor to anyone blessed enough to be touched by her. I call her my guardian angel on Earth as she is always watching over me.

My accomplishments are a direct result of what Mom taught me. There is a saying that behind every successful man is an amazing woman.

For me that woman isn't a wife; it's my mom. I love how humble she is through Christ. She helps people through her charities, and she blesses everyone in her life. You will never see her looking for validation for helping others, she just does it out of the amazing love in her heart.

For as long as I can remember, she has adopted families at Christmas making sure they have presents. Whenever I need help with my angels, it is my mom who is the first to donate. I strive to be just like her in the charity world as, in the past, I was looking for atta boys for my work. She does it like Jesus asks us to do it.

Without her strength and guidance, there is a good chance I would not be here to write these words. The world gives so much attention to me as XFactor, but my mom is the true XFactor behind the scenes. I thank God for placing her as my mom and I am forever grateful, thankful, and blessed because of her.

"As one whom his mother comforts, so I will comfort you."
Isaiah 66:13

"She opens her mouth with wisdom, and the
teaching of kindness is on her tongue."
Proverbs 31:26

Dad

My relationship with my dad can be summarized as best friends. After my parents were divorced, he took me to do things I loved doing. He was an extremely hard-working man who partied just as hard when off the clock.

At age 8, he gave me my first job helping him at his gas station. He loves to fish and he loves our Chiefs. These two things made our relationship strong. Dad wasn't the parent who disciplined me; he was my best friend who bailed me out of situations.

In my teenage years, I fell in love with the drinking and partying lifestyle … just like my dad. Our relationship became one of partying together. Other than friends, he was the only one who supported my partying lifestyle. Even though I was underage, it was all right to drink as long as I was under his supervision.

I strived to earn his approval and make him proud of me. We both struggled with expressing our feelings, especially when we drank. Becoming a Chiefs Superfan was a direct result of my dad. I watched my first game at 3 months old on his lap. He had me every Sunday, so during football season, our day totally revolved around the Chiefs.

When I started going to Arrowhead without my dad, it was the first time he wasn't with me during the game. I would call him before and after the games so we could still have that connection. I started painting my body red and yellow and dressing up in hopes he would see me on TV and fill the void of not having him with me.

In 2000 I wanted my dad to go with me to River Falls to training camp. I called his boss and said, "If he can't go, then I'm putting in his two-weeks' notice." My dad would never take a day off work. His boss said, "Please take him for two weeks. He needs to take some time off." This started a 13-year tradition of Dad going with me to training camp and to Canton, Ohio for the Hall of Fame ceremonies. We made some great memories together doing what we loved most, Chiefs and fishing. All the coaches, players and fans started calling him Daddy X. Being able to experience something that most people don't meant the world to me.

The XFactor of alcohol was always a big part of our time together, especially in River Falls. It seemed like everyone drank in Wisconsin every day, all day long, so our partying seemed normal. But in all honesty, it caused us not to be able to cherish what we were blessed to be doing together.

In the 1990's I got my dad to come to the playoff games, but when he started going to training camp, his trips to Arrowhead increased. He started going to 2-3 games a year with me. We partied so hard together and never slept during these trips. He loved everything about River Falls, as it was small like our hometown. When they moved training camp to St Joseph, he stopped going. But even after the Chiefs moved, he continued to go to games until his health didn't allow it.

I miss all the things we did together as father and son when it comes to Chiefs. For most of my years as a Superfan, I tried to accomplish big things so my dad would be proud of me. Our drinking was XFactor, which didn't allow us to express how much we loved each other. My struggles centered around chemicals, which I inherited from my dad. His good traits that I inherited now outshine those old demons. And we still fish together every chance we get.

Without my dad's love for the Chiefs, I would not have become XFactor. My desire to make him proud drove my passion and I'm forever grateful for that. Sure, chemicals were native XFactor's in our lives, but our love and passion were extremely powerful X0Factors.

I know my dad is proud of my accomplishments. I wouldn't change anything in our relationship because it helped me get to where I am today. Daddy X moved me to extraordinary heights that I could never have imagined. It's such a blessing to call my dad my best friend.

> *"Listen to your father, who gave you life, and do*
> *not despise your mother when she is old."*
> Proverbs 23:22

Stepdad

So many people go without one or both parents in their lives. I'm blessed to have a stepdad who instantly treated me like I was his son.

Early on, our relationship was rocky as he tried to instill rules to make me successful. I rebelled against this. Our relationship started to grow when I went to treatment, as he had also struggled with alcohol in his younger years.

He was one of the best running backs in Kansas during his high school years. We talked sports even though his favorite team was the Broncos. Having a relationship where we rooted for different teams helped me learn how to treat opposing fans. Just because people root for different teams doesn't mean they are unlovable. He also introduced me to golf, which became our favorite father/son activity.

Having him available during my accomplishments and through my tough times has been a blessing. I wasn't his biological child, and he didn't have to treat me like his own, but he did. He has been a great blessing to my mom, too, allowing her to be our family's rock.

If my life's journey ever leads me to being a stepfather, I want to be just like mine!

"I will be a father to him, and he'll be a son to me. When he does wrong, I'll discipline him in the usual ways, the pitfalls and obstacles of this mortal life. But I'll never remove my gracious love from him."
2 Samuel 7:14-15

CHAPTER 9

Addiction

Millions upon millions of people are consumed by addictions. We lose many each year to this disease. One of the main purposes of writing this book is so others can gain hope and inspiration from my story. This is where I share my life as an addict no matter how much pain it involves. If one life can be saved, writing this book is worth it.

I took my first drink when I was still in diapers. At that time, it was acceptable for dads at BBQs to let their kids have a sip of beer. The first time I got drunk was when I was 8 years old with boys who were around 14. I was instantly hooked on the feeling and liked being "cool" by drinking.

Growing up in Scott City, a town of 3,000, there wasn't much to do, so everything surrounding alcohol seemed fun. When I turned 14, my dad would buy me beer, and it would be all right to drink if I was with him. We loved to fish together, and beer was always a part of our fishing trips. When I was in high school, he allowed me to throw parties at his house because at least I wouldn't be out getting in trouble or, even worse, hurt in a wreck. This made me extremely popular in school. People wanted to be my friend because I could get them alcohol. Girls liked me because I was the party boy and party host.

As a freshman in high school, I was only 5'4 and 100 lbs. I wore the ugliest glasses as I had bad eyes since birth. I was extremely insecure due to this, and alcohol took that away and made me feel like I was somebody special.

My addiction to one-night stands began during this time. During junior year, my best friend scored a bag of weed. We went to the country to smoke it, as back then it was so taboo. I had a rush from doing something illegal, which led me to adding Ecstasy and acid in high school.

Then I started getting into trouble with the law. Most of the time they would take our beer and tell us to go home, but I still got 3 minors in possession and three open container tickets.

Since I worked on my granddad's farm, my dad's mechanic shop, and repairing elevators, I'd pay lawyers to make my problems go away. The summer after graduation, I got a DUI. I was hosting a party at my dad's house and went to the gas station to get cigarettes. I was pulled over for having a headlight out by a police officer who had been watching my party. I had major problems with this cop and in the jail cell I struck him. To get out of trouble, I agreed to go to treatment for a month at Valley Hope. I learned about addiction, but I told myself I wasn't like the others because they were all older and had lost everything. I basically wanted to get myself out of trouble, which happened as the courts dropped all charges. Once again, I manipulated the system.

A couple of months before, eight of my buddies went to prom together. Later that night, we decided to host a party at the lake. I wrecked my car by taking a 90 degree turn at 75 mph. I almost went into the lake and barely missed a huge tree that would have killed me and my buddies. This was my second wreck in 2 months, as I had previously wrecked my mom's car. Neither time was I charged with DUI because I didn't report accidents until the next day after I sobered up.

I chose to attend Barton County Community College for two reasons. First, they had a great golf program, and second, it was only two hours from my hometown. College was about freedom to party; it was never about learning. I would party all week and then go home to throw parties on the weekends.

I was introduced to cocaine and other drugs while in college. Cocaine became my choice drug along with alcohol because they made me feel like Superman. Doing cocaine also provided sexual desires as many girls wanted to have sex after doing coke.

During childhood, I worked extremely hard and saved my money. Once I started doing cocaine, I burnt through my life savings. I met a friend who introduced me to selling weed on campus. I found I could pay for my addictions by rolling joints and selling them individually.

A year after I started selling, I got busted and kicked out of campus housing. I moved into town with a friend and that's when partying started 24 hours a day. I had a place where I could throw parties every day and students could come to party. My cocaine habit was out of control, so my dealer had me run coke to neighboring cities. I made around $2,000 a day, which allowed me to buy whatever I wanted. My parties were legendary with kegs of beer and plenty of drugs readily available.

I went through girls as fast as I changed my underwear. I was addicted to seeing how many girls I could sleep with. I would drink all day and night. When I got tired, I would do a couple of lines of cocaine to keep going. I became a big enough enterprise that I hired a couple of friends to sell for me. This only meant more money to fulfill my party lifestyle. A problem arose when the KBI started parking on my block and watching activities going on at the house. One day a friend, who had recently been busted for drugs, came by. He knew I didn't sell cocaine to anyone; I just ran huge loads. I opened his shirt and he was wearing a wire.

Later that day, I packed up $55,000 and went back home to work for my grandfather on the farm. Two weeks later, I was pulled over for another DUI. This time there was no manipulating the court and I was convicted of my first DUI offense. The rest of the summer, my cocaine habit blew through $55,000. The first night I was back in Great Bend, someone broke into my house. I cocked my 12 gauge shotgun and pointed at the shadow I saw, and they ran out of my house. This was the final sign that I needed to get out of the drug game, as I knew it was only going to end with me going to the pen or dead.

I found a job at a handicapped facility which gave me enough money to drink and throw parties, but I didn't have enough for my cocaine habit. So, I slowed down on cocaine unless someone brought it to the party. I worked the midnight shift so I would drink until about 10 p.m., take a nap, and go to work while the party continued at my house. Every morning I would drink until I became sleepy, as that was the only way I could sleep during the day. The next summer, I got another DUI. I did a diversion like I had the previous summer so there weren't many consequences for my actions.

I was good at working with individuals with disabilities, so promotions kept coming my way. I eventually became a Residential Manager working over 100 hours a week and throwing parties whenever I wasn't at work. One night, my buddies bet me I couldn't be with just one girl for a month, and a keg of beer was the wager. I won that bet and, for the first time in my life, I fell in love. She changed my life and, over the next three years, she got me to change. We were best friends and drank together daily. and I was monogamous. Over time, she became jealous and swore I was cheating on her; alcohol does that by making us paranoid.

Eventually I got my butt kicked by her ex-boyfriend and our relationship ended. The night we broke up, I met a stripper which started an off and on relationship that lasted the next 15 years, which always centered around drugs and alcohol. She had a five-year-old son named Tyler whom I adopted as my own. After about a year together, we found out she was pregnant and since her livelihood was dancing, she had an abortion, with my consent. Killing my first child was the hardest thing I've ever done. The day we went to the abortion clinic in Wichita, I cried. It broke my heart watching around twenty girls lined up like cattle going to the slaughter. Still, to this day, I wish I could have convinced her to have the child. It was her body and her decision. This experience led me and her back to using hard drugs to cope with the pain. Our relationship was torn apart, and I started cheating on her. Eventually, the relationship ended and I asked her to move out.

The house I had was too expensive for me to afford alone so I decided that my two drug dealers should move in. The partying started again. I used cocaine daily and started smoking crack. Instead of one relationship, I went back to having many. I slept with five girls from work that I was manager over. My life spun out of control and, once again, the KBI started parking on my block.

After meeting a girl that I really liked, I told the five girls from work I wouldn't be dating them anymore. This made one of them extremely mad and she told my boss that I had been sleeping with the five of them. I was fired the next day, and my roommates started paying me more for allowing them to deal from my house. For the next 3 months, I partied like Charlie Sheen.

I was heading to a Chiefs game to do Spider man when I got word that my house was about to be raided. When I returned home, it was completely destroyed. My roommates had thrown parties while I was gone. People had defecated all over the house, broken the windows, and burnt my cabinets in the fireplace. In addition, they either stole or ruined my possessions. I cried because I had lost everything, and I called my dad and asked if I could come back home until I could get back on my feet. After moving home, my drinking got worse.

I was hired as a supervisor to work at a handicapped facility in Garden City, but being back with my high school friends, we threw more parties, which were attended mostly by high school kids. I bought alcohol for minors and engaged in activities with my old friends that I should not have. This was a dark time of my life, as I partied nonstop whenever I wasn't at work. I was a bad role model. I was unhappy and jumped from relationship to relationship, sometimes dating more than one at a time.

On one of my trips home from watching the Chiefs, I wrecked my car. I was taking a back highway and fell asleep at the wheel, rolling my car and driving off a curve. I awoke in the back seat with blood all over me from the broken glass. God was definitely with me because, honestly, I should have died in that wreck. But then, my drinking intensified because of my unhappiness.

In 2002, my best friend from my hometown asked me to move with him to Manhattan, Kansas. He said, "All you're doing is wasting your life away in Scott City. A new place will allow you to leave your demons behind." But my problems followed me. Moving to a college town gave me new parties and more exciting bars to go to. Then I took a job caring for Kyle, who had muscular dystrophy, and also got hired as a supervisor for another handicapped facility. Working two jobs meant having more money, which was spent at bars or strip clubs. I was a functioning alcoholic, but the only drug I was using was marijuana.

My roommate met a girl he wanted to move in, so I moved out and was just a block away from the college bar scene. Instead of drinking mostly at home, I started going to bars seven days a week. Because of my drinking, I couldn't afford the rent, so I put an ad in paper. A mom called me saying her son had just gotten out of jail and needed a place to live, so I let him move in. Two weeks later, he had a lot of money, even though he wasn't working. A couple of days later, my old roommate called to let me know that SWAT had just raided our house. Come to find out, this guy was holding people up at ATMs. He had also committed armed robbed at McDonald's, Burger King, and Sonic.

I moved in with my best friend who was a bartender at my favorite bar. After just a couple of months, SWAT raided my house again. My new roommate had set the pawn shop on fire where he was working. He had initially told us that four black guys had robbed it, shot him in arm, and set it on fire. The cameras in the parking lot told a different story. What are the chances of having two roommates who did those crazy things in just two months?

Not much later, Kyle died and my drinking spiraled out of control. I decided that my time was done in Manhattan and, with things growing with the Chiefs, it was time to move to KC. I moved into an enormous house with a buddy who loved to party. It didn't take long before I added drugs to the alcohol. We threw parties, but this is when I started to realize that my drinking and drugs were abnormal. That was because all of my friends were either married or had kids.

In KC, I had more girls at my disposal so my addiction to girls returned in full force. I said I'd never settle down with one girl because having many was more fun. Truth is, I probably didn't want any girl to get to know me too well, because I always figured they would try to change me.

One night I met some friends at a bar and, on the way home, got pulled over for not using the blinker. After another sobriety test, I was found to be driving drunk again, so I got another DUI. Just two months later, I went to a huge Chiefs away game party at 810 Sports Bar. On the way home, I got pulled over for having a tag light out. I got my second DUI in just two months. I hired a lawyer and, though there was a great chance I could beat the last DUI, the day we went in for trial I got horrible news. They had changed the law and the two DUI's I had done diversions on 15 years earlier would now count. I was facing my fourth DUI.

I thought that since I had paid double fines and done community service, they were permanently removed from my record. But instead of facing misdemeanor, I was facing a felony. An arrest warrant had be issued for this felony, so I had to turn myself in and bond out. When I posted bond, I found out they wouldn't release me because the judge had ordered me to be on house arrest as part of the bond. I felt like I had been proven guilty before I was even found guilty in the courtroom.

On house arrest, I could only leave my house to go to work for eight hours a day. They also put a breathalyzer in my house which I had to blow in whenever my phone rang from house arrest. I lost my job at a handicapped facility due to my license being suspended, so I took the first job I could find that didn't require a driver's license. A blessing was that it ended my drinking and drug use and gave me time to build my charity organization, KCSuperfans.

After six months on house arrest, I took a plea deal and pled guilty. I wanted to fight this, but being in house arrest was financially breaking me, and being constantly stuck at home was horrible. It was almost time for training camp, and the Chiefs games were about to start back up. I wasn't going to miss that. I received ten days in jail as part of my plea, which was the first time I had stayed in jail more than a few hours.

For the next two years, I had random UAs at least once a week while on probation. I was able to stay clean for another six months after getting off probation. This two and half years clean was by far the longest I had stayed clean since I was a young kid. It was a forced clean though, as I knew I would go to jail for a long time if I was ever caught drinking. When clean, I got into a serious relationship. Then I was blessed with my amazing daughter. The relationship, however, was extremely toxic. I was constantly accused of cheating and fighting daily was dragging me down. In my past relationships, I would leave if drama happened, but I wanted to be available for my daughter and her older sister, who I had accepted as mine.

Many times, I would say, "I can't live in this hell anymore," but my kids would bring me back. One day after dealing with my significant other while I was at work, I stopped at a BBQ restaurant before going home to fight with her. At the restaurant, I struck up a conversation with a man whose wife was also causing drama. He said, "Let me buy you a beer." I responded, "You know what? I haven't had one in over two and half years, but that sounds really good."

This started a cycle of stopping in every night to get buzzed so I could cope with the fights at home. My significant other got an overnight job which allowed me to drink beer while she was at work. I still took care of the kids, but my alcoholism returned full force.

One morning my partner brought cocaine home from work. We started using it together and for once we didn't fight. Instantly, I was again addicted to cocaine which I had been able to fight off for years. Not long after, I learned she was cheating on me with the man supplying her with cocaine. This was the last straw so after years of cheating, lies and the worst relationship of my life, I walked away for the last time, which felt like freedom from being in jail.

But not having my daughter and to hide the pain, I went beyond crazy with partying and turned to alcohol and cocaine harder than ever. The next two years I would drink a thirty pack a day and, when I would get tired, I would do cocaine to stay up. My drug habit grew to an eight ball of cocaine every two days. My life, job, charity work and relationships suffered tremendously. I was a horrible father because I didn't have extra money to take my daughter to do fun things when I had her. Our weekends were spent at home so I could drink. I tried to hide my addictions from others, but people closest to me knew the truth.

One morning my mom, dad, aunt, and friends showed up to do an intervention. I had been wanting to quit and stop the insanity. Every time I tried, my mountain of problems would overwhelm me, and I would use drugs and alcohol to forget. I decided to go to a treatment center in western Kansas so I could be close to my family.

My daughter was my biggest motivation, as she deserved a better father than I had been. The next five years, I was able to stay sober, and an amazing accomplishment happened. My addiction turned to helping others and my charity organization was restored to the way it once was. I met the most amazing kids and made a huge difference in their lives.

I relapsed on my birthday, May 8th, 2017, when I lost my angel, Aimee. The next two months were the worst times of my life. (I share this in the spiritual warfare chapter later in this book.) I was arrested for a warrant on July 30th, 2017, and spent the next 10 days in jail. No one would bond me out in fear I would die. It was the scariest time, as I was thrown in the hole with a few murderers. Since I was the only white person in the hole, they attacked me.

After getting a Bible in my cell, I began to read. One morning I hit my knees for the first time, asking God to give me a glimmer of hope. That's how far addiction had destroyed my life; I had lost everything, including hope. In just two months, the devil stripped me of everything I had.

God put on my heart that he would restore me, but I had to quit using the chemicals the devil was poisoning me with. I've been clean since July 30th, 2017. It's no coincidence that when devastation happened, I made chemicals my number one XFactor. On the flip side, my greatest victories come when I pursue my new number one XFactor, Jesus, and our Father in Heaven.

Few people are able to use alcohol and drugs like I did and live to talk about it. In the last 10 years, I know 100 people who have relapsed into drugs and alcohol, and that decision has cost them their lives. For many years, the only prayer I had was, "God, please get me out of this, and I promise not to do it again." The scary prayers, though, were when I prayed, "God, take me in my sleep because I can't go on."

I am grateful that God didn't answer those prayers. I needed to go through my consequences and I'm so thankful I'm still alive to live in

God's glory. I'm thankful, grateful and blessed that God protected me and kept me alive through it all. I will live my life to glorify him in everything I do so that I can repay him.

"Let us then approach God's throne of grace with confidence,
so that we may receive mercy and find grace
to help us in our time of need."
Hebrews 4:16

"Have mercy on me, O God,
according to your unfailing love;
according to your great compassion
blot out my transgressions.
Wash away all my iniquity
and cleanse me from my sin."
Psalm 51:1-2

"Remember, Lord, your great mercy and love
for they are from of old.
Do not remember the sins of my youth
and my rebellious ways;
according to your love remember me,
for you, Lord, are good."
Psalm 25:6-7

CHAPTER 10

Hall of Fame

As a kid, I dreamed of becoming a professional athlete. I would practice basketball, football, baseball, or golf as though I was going against my sports heroes on TV. Sports was one of biggest influences in my life that motivated me to strive for greatness.

Sports taught me valuable lessons in working on my skills so I could do my part to make my teams successful. Sports taught me to have faith in my teammates and to work together to achieve victory. Sports taught me discipline, faith, what passion could achieve, and how hard work would pay off in the end.

At a young age, I watched my heroes being inducted in the Hall of Fame. I realized in college that I didn't have enough talent to make it professionally, but when I became a Superfan, it made me feel like I could play a role and impact the game on the field.

After being a Superfan for years, I had separated myself as a different fan than most. My houses, vehicles, clothes, tattoos, charity work, etc., were matched by few fans. I was a 24/7/365 fan whose life revolved around football. My mentor, Arrowman, and then my Superfan teammate, Weirdwolf, were inducted into the Visa Hall of Fans in Canton, Ohio. Visa had partnered with Pro Football Hall of

Fame to induct a fan from each team every year. I didn't know about it until WeirdWolf was inducted.

In 2003, there was another HOF contest. To enter, I had to write a 500 word essay, which was tough. How could I explain everything with so few words? I asked an English teacher to help me make it powerful and cut out all unnecessary words. When I sent my essay, I was beyond nervous. Would they think I was worthy of representing my beloved team in the Hall Of Fame? The next 3 months were stressful as I awaited news of whether I was selected.

One day, the voting committee called and did a 30-minute phone interview. They told me that I was a finalist and they would be making their decision in two weeks. My anticipation was so high as I dreamed of what my life would be like if I was selected. Then one day while I was in the bank, my phone rang from a strange area code. The voice on the other end asked, "Is this Ty Rowton, aka XFactor?" I answered, "Yes, it is." They said, "Congratulations! You have been selected in the 2003 Visa Hall of Fame." I was pretty much speechless, but managed to say, "Thank you so much."

The bank teller asked, "Are you all right, Ty?" She thought something tragic had happened. When I answered, "I was just inducted into the Pro Football Hall of Fame," she screamed, "Oh my god, congratulations." A party started inside the bank with employees and customers. Everyone wanted to be the first to get pictures and autographs with the newest member of the HOF.

I cried happy tears, reflecting on things in my life and thanking God for this honor. After leaving the bank, I went straight to the liquor store and bought a 12 pack. Then I drove to my favorite fishing spot. I spent the next 12 hours calling everyone to give them this great news. I remember thinking, "I'm a Hall of Famer now so I must raise my game." (That didn't happen until I gave my life to Christ.)

The Hall of Fame had always been my ultimate dream. The next months were crazy with interviews, which were more than I had done my entire life. Everyone was excited and treated me differently. I heard, "You are the only person I've ever met who is in the Hall of Fame."

In December, my family and friends accompanied me to the Chiefs game against the Lions. I was honored at halftime on the 50-yard line in front of 80,000 fans. I was invited to stand on the sidelines during the first half, behind my heroes, which was the first time I had been on the field on game day. All the players throughout the first half came and congratulated me, as Priest had let them know what was happening at halftime.

I was blessed to be so close to this team through all my charity work and experiences at training camp. They were beyond happy for me and said, "You deserve this buddy." As halftime approached, it felt like I was living a dream. The founder of Team Priest, Christopher Bush, was escorting me. I told him, "Make sure to catch me if I faint or wobble." I asked him to walk me to the 50-yard line and to stay with me during this experience.

Upon getting to the 50-yard line, the Chiefs started a 60-second tribute video showing me on the jumbotrons. I had no clue. Tears of happiness streamed down my face. A representative from the Hall of Fame gave me an exact replica plaque that was like the ones hanging in Canton. Goosebumps went down my body when the crowded stadium stood up, cheering and clapping. I finally experienced what the players do. A feeling like I had never felt vibrated throughout my whole body. So many of the fans in attendance didn't know I was being inducted into the Hall of Fame. Leaving the field, my whole family was in row 1 of the 50-yard line, tears filling their eyes. It meant the world to have them there to support me.

The rest of the day, I was mobbed by fans hugging me and saying how proud they were. I shed tears nonstop that day. I had never received so much love from so many people in one day. I remember thinking, "Wow, very few people get to experience this."

It meant the world being a small-town boy and knowing that it would give hope to others that dreams can come true if they put their mind to it. I had come a long way from being a small town boy from the Midwest to receiving the highest honor in football. Still, to this day, people get excited about me being in the Hall of Fame. It is such an honor to represent millions of Chiefs fans across the world.

I thought this would be the ultimate accomplishment, but God was preparing me for bigger things. You might want to grab a few tissues as the next part about my granddad and the Hall of Fame may bring tears to your eyes.

"Thine, O Lord, is the greatness, and the power, and the glory,
and the victory, and the majesty: for all that is in the heaven and
in the earth is thine; thine is the kingdom, O Lord,
and thou art exalted as head above all."
1 Chronicles 29:11

"O sing unto the Lord a new song; For he hath done marvelous things:
His right hand, and his holy arm, hath gotten him the victory."
Psalm 98:1

CHAPTER 11

My Granddad and the Hall of Fame

At two weeks old, I rode the combine during harvest with my granddad. He held me in one arm and drove the combine with the other. I was his first grandchild, and he loved me so much; he said I was a happy baby while in his arms in the combine. My granddad was the hardest working man I knew, complete with the biggest heart. His sense of humor was unmatched, and I laughed at his jokes. As a kid, I would go to the farm every chance I got. My grandma was equally loving and spoiled me. I also had an uncle who did fun activities with me. I rode the combine with him every harvest, which are some of my favorite memories.

In high school I went to work for my granddad on the farm. He taught me every aspect of taking seeds and then nurturing them so they could feed more people than I could imagine. My granddad was passionate about farming. It was passed down from his father who was a pioneer in an untamed land.

Most people in my hometown stayed to take over their family farms and didn't go into the world to chase their dreams. When I left home, he became my biggest fan. He would ask everyone, "Do you know the Chiefs Superfan Spider Man and the XFactor?" If they said yes, he would say, "That's my grandson." If not, he would explain who I was.

When I called my grandparents, he would ask, "Are you still wearing your PJs in front of millions?" He loved teasing me, but he was also proud that I followed my dreams.

Granddad and Grandma were the first people I called when I got news that I was being inducted into the Hall of Fame. They were excited and proud of me. It was a blessing to have them at Arrowhead, at their first professional game, when I was inducted. As I walked off the field, my heart melted as I saw them crying with pure happiness.

A few months later, I received a call that my hero, my granddad, had pancreatic cancer. I always thought that somehow, he would beat it. He was strongest man I knew. In high school he broke every bone in his back and was told he would never walk again. But after a year, he overcame that and proved the doctors wrong. He had survived the Great Depression and the dust bowl. How would cancer be any different? I had complete faith that he would beat it. But as I watched his body deteriorate to skin and bones, I knew he wouldn't.

At the end of July, I went to River Falls for the Chiefs Training Camp. After arriving, I found out Granddad had been hospitalized and time was closing in on him. The last night in River Falls before heading to Canton to be inducted, I called my mom. I could sense something was terribly wrong. I told them I was coming home. They said, "No. It means so much to Granddad for you to be inducted. You must do that for him."

The next morning, I called my family and told them I was getting my plaque and giving my speech. I wanted to know the truth about Granddad's condition. Mom said, "Your Granddad has gone into a coma, and the doctors can't believe he made it through the night." I told her, "I'm coming home as soon as I get my plaque." She answered, "No, Ty. He won't be alive by the time you get here. He would be so mad if you drove without sleep. Heaven forbid that you get into an accident. That would devastate the family even more."

At the ceremony, I asked my fellow Superfans if I could speak first and told them about the circumstances. As tears streamed down my face, I told everyone I was accepting the award on behalf of my biggest fan, my granddad, who was on his death bed. Then I jumped into the car and started the 18 hour drive home. I called to let the family know and they told Granddad, "Hang on! Ty Lee is coming home."

That was the longest trip of my life. I only stopped to get gas, use the restroom, and grab caffeine. I called every hour and my family would put the phone up to Granddad's ear so he could hear my voice. The next morning, I arrived at the hospital in my hometown. I was the last family member to get there, and the whole family started crying when I walked into the room. I went to my granddad's side, grabbed his hand and kissed him on forehead. I said, "Granddad, it's your grandson, Ty Lee. I just got back from Canton, Ohio and didn't accept the HOF award for myself. I accepted it for my hero, which is you, Granddad. So forever we will be in the Pro Football Hall of Fame together. Granddad, it's alright, you can now go to heaven. I look around this room and see the most amazing family you have created. Your work on Earth is finished, and your legacy lives in us." He squeezed my hand to let me know he heard me. A couple of minutes later, he took his last breath as I held his hand in mine.

If you ever question whether people can hear when in a coma, there's your answer. My granddad fought off death until I could get to him. Still, when I tell this story, I cry. My granddad was one of the biggest XFactor's in my life. The things he taught me not only benefit me but everyone I encounter. He is always with me as I know he is my guardian angel. From a field of dreams in the middle of nowhere to Canton, Ohio! What a great journey we had together!

"Then the angel showed me the river of the water of life, bright as crystal, flowing from the throne of God and of the Lamb through the middle of the street of the city; also, on either side of the river, the tree of life with its twelve kinds of fruit, yielding its fruit each month. The leaves of the tree were for the healing of the nations. No longer will there be anything accursed, but the throne of God and of the Lamb will be in it, and his servants will worship him. They will see his face, and his name will be on their foreheads. And night will be no more. They will need no light of lamp or sun, for the Lord God will be their light, and they will reign forever and ever."

Revelation 22:1-5

CHAPTER 12

70 Straight Hours of Football

In 2007, I went to a tailgate party at Arrowhead. A representative from Dish Network approached my apprentice and me about entering the Ultimate Chiefs Fan contest. So, we did.

A week later, I got a call that I was one of two finalists. A few minutes later, my apprentice called. I had never heard him so excited. He had received a call saying that he was a finalist in the Dish Network Contest. He had called work to take time off so he could go to Denver. The challenge was to compete to set a Guinness World Record for watching football. He asked me to support him and get the Chiefs fans to call him to keep him awake. My response completely crashed his world. I said, "Congrats! I just received the same call, so I know who you are competing with."

I heard his excitement leave. He knew they would pick me because I had been doing it longer. I answered, "No matter who they pick, we need to support one another. If they pick me and I win the grand prize, I will take you to the Pro Bowl in Hawaii."

The next day, I was chosen to represent Chiefs. I would fly to Denver in two days to try to set a new world record for watching football. The previously held record was 62 hours and held by a Canadian man. The

Chiefs were playing on the road, so I didn't have to worry about missing that game – I had not missed a game since the 1990s, and my streak was important to me. The night before the competition, I was too excited to sleep. So, when the competition started, I had already been awake for 8 hours.

The competition started at 8 a.m. on Sunday morning against seven other fans from the NFL Dish Network Markets. We were assigned 2 girls who would work 4-hour shifts watching us. Their only job was to make sure we didn't take our eyes off the TV; if we did, we would be instantly disqualified. We would also be disqualified if we closed our eyes longer than normal blinks. As I sat in my brand-new lazy boy chair, I realized how hard this was going to be.

We could order anything to eat or drink from the bar. I knew food would make me tired so I had my assistants order whatever they wanted and I would take a couple bites. I ordered Orange Juice because I knew it would give me natural energy without crashes. The other contestants were drinking pop and energy drinks.

The girls who spent 4-hour shifts with me had fun and requested to always be with me. To be fair, though, they had to rotate. After everyone sat with me, they did drawings to see who chose me. I told every girl, "For the next 4 hours, we are going to have a party. We can talk about anything you choose." I won't lie. Girls got a little naughty with me and vice versa.

I asked the girls to answer incoming phone calls and then hand me the phone so I could keep my eyes on the TV. My friends were posting my phone number and updates on the Chiefs message boards. After a while, I was receiving calls from fans all over the world. Chiefs play-ers who were my friends also called to encourage me. This blew away the girls who were helping me. They would say, "Is this the real.......?" Talking to fans from all over the world kept me distracted from how tired I was. It also encouraged me to know it meant so much to so many people, and I couldn't let them down.

When games weren't on, we watched the NFL network, one of the official sponsors, or a football movie. Being the only dressed up Superfan, most of the media wanted to speak to me. I was doing interviews with news stations all over America. CNN was doing hourly reports on our progress. The news stations loved interviewing me as I was constantly cracking jokes.

Someone suggested we have a contest to see who could go the longest without a restroom break. I made it 18 hours and won. When asked how I did it, I jokingly responded, "I was wearing Depends and then the catheter took over when my diaper was full."

After 18 hours of competing, one contestant dropped out. At around 48 hours, I started seeing stars, like I was on an acid trip, which I had been on many times in my life. We got a five-minute break every hour or we could bank that time. The other contestants used banked minutes to take naps, but I vowed that I would not sleep until I set the world record. Around the 60th hour, my buddy from Indy started fading fast. I encouraged him to get up and exercise with me to get his blood pumping. I shouted out to the team, "Let's work together to set the world record. A Canadian owns this record, and football is our National past time, not Canada's. I want to show the world our teamwork, sportsmanship, and friendship. Let's team up, encourage one another, and set a new world record together. We can turn off the televisions together at the 70 hour mark, leaving it in Dish Network and the NFL Network's hand to decide the winner."

About an hour later, we were told by sponsors that they were amazed by this decision, and if we made it 70 hours, everyone would get the grand prize. At this time, I decided to take a 3 hour break and go to a nearby bar with girls who had been with me. Some of the girls scheduled their time off to go with me. As I walked into the bar, the DJ saw me and said, "Did you set the Guinness World Record, XFactor?" I answered, "I'm about 7 hours away from the new mark, but we have already broken the existing record." Everyone in the bar cheered, and lots of Bronco's fans congratulated and bought energy drinks for me."

An amazing transformation had happened since the contest started. At the start, I was seated closest to the fence that blocked people in the bar from coming into our area. Bronco's fans could come 3 feet away from me and taunt me, trying to get me to look away from TV, which so many did. I had been on all the local news stations, and they had learned about my charity organization. Broncos' fans had actually become XFactor fans. During the competition, I also had around 10,000 Chiefs fans in Colorado drive to see me attempting the record. All of this blew me away. This was a big deal to fans all over the world.

After getting back to the competition, I had to push other competitors, as everyone was completely out of gas. Drinking energy drinks was a mistake, as I started crashing from them. The last hour was the toughest and longest hour of my life. A feeling of accomplishment rained over my body as we counted down the last 10 seconds. A huge roar went over the whole bar, and I hugged everyone who was involved. Happy tears streamed from the faces of our teammates, as we had made history together. Deciding not to be selfish and trying to win it all by myself was such a blessing as I made lifelong friends. I was ready for sleep, but there were many reporters who had come to interview me. They were limited to only 5 minutes, but I spent the next 3 hours doing interview after interview.

When I finished, I had enough time to get my belongings from the motel and go to airport, where other phone interviews came in. People at the airport had seen me on the news wherever they were, so I was mobbed by people wanting to talk and take pictures.

On the plane ride home, there were people from KC who had been to San Diego, so I shared what had happened. After arriving home, I slept for 2 hours before going into the local TV and radio station studios. I had to work a 12-hour shift on Thursday. And Friday was Red Friday for our home opener. I spent the next 3 days making appearances. After getting home from the game on Friday night, I slept for 14 straight hours. (I slept 10 hours total in 8 days.)

The prize for winning the contest was a lazy boy, a flat screen TV, Dish Network for 3 years, 52 cases of Monster energy drink, and a trip for two to the Pro Bowl in Hawaii for 7 days. In total, I won $32,000 worth of prizes. (I learned this wasn't a good thing when I did taxes). I took my apprentice to Hawaii. Even though this was a grand gesture, I sensed this would also make us enemies. (More on that later.)

Though it was the hardest thing I've ever done physically, it instilled in me that I could do anything if I put my mind to it.

"I have fought the good fight, I have finished the race,
I have kept the faith."
2 Timothy 4:7

"He gives strength to the weary and increases the power of the weak.
Even youths grow tired and weary, and young men stumble
and fall; but those who hope in the Lord will renew their
strength. They will soar on wings like eagles; they will run
and not grow weary, they will walk and not be faint."
Isaiah 40:29-31

"Come to me, all you who are weary and burdened,
and I will give you rest."
Matthew 11:28

CHAPTER 13

Charity

Growing up in a small farming community, I experienced our small town helping those who struggled. My family, through businesses, donated money and time to help any cause. I was inspired by my mom helping others.

When I started working with disabled individuals, it exposed me to fundraising activities. I was inspired by the late Chiefs owner, Lamar Hunt, not only by how much he helped, but also how he inspired players to have their own charity organizations. When I was dressing up as Spider man for Andre Rison, I was on a platform where I could get involved with the Chiefs players and community events.

My favorite player, Derrick Thomas (DT), was the founder of Third and Long. One day, two weeks before the crash that eventually took his life, I was visiting a tailgate next to the players parking lot. A fan said, "Spider man, a player is calling for you." I walked to the car and was greeted by DT and his amazing smile. I went into shock. He said, "Give the Raiders hell today. We need you." I laughed and said, "No, you give them hell. We need you to do what you always do against the Raiders." He answered, "Well, together we will give them hell." Then I added, "I'm so glad you re-signed with the Chiefs for the rest of your career." And his last words to me were, "I will be a Chief for life. I got to go." I still remember those words. He fulfilled that promise and is now a Chief in Heaven.

My charity activity took a step up when Priest Holmes created Team Priest. I was selected as the first fan of the week and highlighted on their website. Eventually I was invited to every event they did to impact the community. I saw firsthand the need and how a few people can make an impact.

I became best friends with Christoper Bush who ran Team Priest. Our skin color was opposite, but we called each other brothers. We would do fun things together and then celebrate afterwards. I partied harder than Chris, as he was the responsible one. We led a caravan of Chiefs fans to St. Louis for a preseason game. My friends who went with me thought this was the greatest opportunity ever. For three days, we didn't sleep and we partied like rock stars. It ended with a party back in KC where I was to judge an ultimate fan contest. Watching the video the next day, I was embarrassed by how drunk I was in front of hundreds of fans. I vowed that I would not do that again.

During this time, Priest got me thinking. His nickname for me was Sexy X. Priest said, "Ty, we both have platforms. You have a bigger platform than you realize. You have two different sides. I see one side when you are at events bringing so much joy to others. The other side is the party boy. Sure, you are the life of the party, but that doesn't impact others. With your platform, more people see and hear the things you do and say. The problem is those two worlds can't coincide for very long. There will be a day when you have to choose between being a role model or being a party boy." Priest was right. I did godly things, but the devil said, "It's all right to party because you do so many things for others."

A few years later, I was invited to a Priests charity golf tournament. Afterward, Priest started speaking to the people in attendance. His words made me cry in front of hundreds. Priest said, "I'm so happy

XFactor came today. It means the world to me to have a friend like him. Whenever I ask Ty to help with a cause, he drops everything and shows up. Ty even leaves work and drives two hours one way at the drop of a hat. I seriously don't think XFactor ever sleeps. I think he must feel like a proud father because he has taken my dream of Team Priest and added it to his charity, KCSuperfans."

Little did Priest know, but Chris had asked me not to drink at the event. I literally was rock bottom and that was the only sober day I had in years. The tears were from embarrassment because all of the wonderful things he said about me were far from how I felt about myself.

In 2003, inspired by Team Priest, I called Weirdwolf and Arrowman. "We are all doing different charity activities. How about we team up and help each other?" Arrowman suggested that when I got inducted into the Hall of Fame, we sit down with Hogettes from Washington, DC. They had raised millions of dollars for charities.

After meeting with them in Canton, we had an idea of how to form our charity group, KCSuperfans. Weirdwolf and I also brought on board our two apprentices. The first meeting was mostly about throwing a huge party for kids. Once we launched KCSuperfans, that idea went out the window because we were overwhelmed by all the charities that wanted our help. Every event we went to, people from other charities invited us to their events.

We were approached by a teacher who wanted to use us in her new reading program she was creating for her school. She wrote a program that allowed kids to get a first down for every book they read, and classes could learn teamwork by competing against other classes in their grade. We went to a launch party to get kids excited at the beginning of the year and then came back at the end of the year to hand out prizes.

We also found an artist to make comic books that we could take to the school. That project never got funded, but we found teammates who would come to every event and draw for all the kids. Soon we had face painters, magicians, and tons of volunteers to help us. We also got 3 photographers who went with us to capture all the memories for our website and social media.

Our next project was producing posters that we named the Kids of KC. The first year, we teamed up with Dante Hall and Eddie Kennison to raise money for their charities. We also created personal football cards that we could autograph and give to kids. In 2000, when I started giving those cards out, I saw the smiles they could bring to kids' faces. We quickly learned that it wasn't how much money we could raise but, more importantly, our role was to bring happiness to so many.

Soon we branched out to make presentations at schools. Arrowman and I set a record for speaking at seven schools in one day. A few years later, I broke that record by speaking at eight schools. My college buddy, Justin, asked for my help as he was at a loss in what else to do. Two kids had committed suicide and there were rumors that a suicide pack had been formed and many more were planning on committing suicide. Justin was the Sheriff and they had tried everything they could think of to stop this.

I prayed that I could make a difference. Never had it been a life-or-death situation surrounding my speeches. Being a county with poverty and a drug problem, I could totally relate with what kids were going through. Justin told me afterward that he was amazed by the kids' reactions. He said, "I sat in the last row at every school. For 45 minutes, you had every single kid's undivided attention. When you moved on stage, every single head followed you. Not one kid was distracted from what you were saying." My speech must have opened the kid's eyes because, to this day, no more suicides have happened. I realized my platform could save lives.

My own actions eventually tore apart KCSuperfans from the top members. When I got a DUI, my apprentice called for me to be removed from the organization I had founded. He was so worried that the media would catch wind and it would give us a bad name in the community. It was also during this time that Arrowman and WeirdWolf decided to retire due to the drama and the time it was taking away from their families.

I decided to remove two other Superfans due to the drama and to start it over being the only well-known Superfan. I still had teammates who helped me, and I found new dress-up Superfans I could mentor. After a while, I began to burn out. Dressing up 200 times a year and constantly on the go ran my batteries down. Even when I didn't want to attend, I felt obligated.

Another project we started in the beginning was having a buddy, Ron, hand paint footballs of us as cartoon characters. I would get footballs autographed by 25-30 players and then donate them to charities to raffle or auction off. These footballs always raised at least $1,000, with one raising over $10,000. At the end, though, the work of going to events where players were to get them autographed was too much. Before 9/11, I could go to the stadium and get them autographed after players got out of practice. Also, I could go to River Falls for training camp and get them signed. After the Chiefs moved their training camp, it became more of a struggle, so after donating 53 footballs, I ended that project.

I also had players to autograph a new XFactor cape each year. That was easier as I didn't have to carry footballs everywhere. I started doing two capes a year and donating them to charities. Most charities that I donated to wanted me to be the runway model and auction the cape off my back. I was blown away by how badly people wanted my capes and how much they would pay charities for them.

For three years, I also raised money to buy 3,000 toys at Christmas for kids who wouldn't get any. Jenna loved helping Daddy shop for these kids. Most of the money I raised came from auctioning off my most prized memorabilia. When I went to Christmas parties for these kids, my heart would melt, and all of my hard work was paid with hugs, love, and smiles.

For five years, I was clean and sober. I reinvented KCSuperfans to become a powerful organization that helped more charities than I could imagine. It had so much success that I decided to call all the biggest Superfans from other teams that were in the HOF with me. We formed what was called Legends of the Stands. I was filled with a new passion. The excitement of building something never built before lit a fire in me. I thought I could turn my day-to-day operations over completely to the secretary of KCSuperfans. She had slowly taken over more and more responsibilities. My time was cut short when I decided to open a sports store by the stadiums. These 3 things had me burning a candle at both ends.

Six months into this, I lost my angel, Aimee, on my birthday. This cast me back into addiction and spiritual warfare. (I have devoted 3 chapters to that.) It affected my two charities in a profound way as I sunk back into addiction and negative activities. I focused my attention on greedy things with the store and a possible National reality show.

The things I did under chemical influences brought negative attention to my charity organizations. I got a call one night from an angel's parents telling me that my secretary had made a public announcement that I had retired from KCSuperfans. On top of that, she had appointed my two former apprentices, who had become my enemies, as faces of my charity organization. In addition, my charity organization wasn't KCSuperfans anymore but Superfans of KC. No longer were kids called angels but now Super kids.

I also learned that all contact information for charities, angels, and media had been removed from my Gmail account. I lost 14 years of information that I ran my charity through. I also found out that every KCSuperfans social media site had been discontinued. This crushed me, as I had trusted her with everything. Shortly after that, the national

Legends of the Stands organization crashed as members didn't want to be associated with all the drama. I decided to walk away from helping charities for a few years and focus on getting clean.

The last few years, I've slowly started helping my angels again. I don't do many enormous charity events anymore but focus on impacting the angels in my life. Before, I was consumed with trying to help the masses. Now I am focused on being XFactor to the ones closest to me. This allows me to impact their lives instead of just touching on a day here and there.

I have always donated items to charities but now I love giving them to these amazing kids. It is not about raising money; many people can do that. My life spent helping others has had its struggles, but it has brought me so much happiness. I'm thankful, grateful, and blessed that God gave me opportunities to meet many wonderful people.

In the past, I looked for recognition of helping others. Now I love doing it because God asks us to do it without anyone knowing. God is glorified and not me. As this world gets crazier and horrible things happen, we can still lend a helping hand. This is how the world will change-- by simply loving each other; especially the ones not as fortunate as we are.

"If you pour yourself out for the hungry and
satisfy the desire of the afflicted,
then shall your light rise in the darkness and
your gloom be as the noonday."
Isaiah 58:10

"In the same way, let your light shine before others,
that they may see your good deeds and glorify your Father in heaven."
Matthew 5:16

CHAPTER 14

Chiefs Everything

One doesn't become a Chiefs Superfan by just being a fan during the season. I wear all Chiefs from head to toe, 365 days a year. The Chiefs play an enormous part of my life, every single day. I love interacting with over 200,000 social media followers talking about our beloved team. I have two completely decked out Chiefs vehicles so everywhere I go, fans are attracted to them. My house is full of everything Chiefs, including my pictures with players for the last 30 years. These are my prized possessions. Every one of them is personally autographed to me and are treasures of all the memories. I currently have six Chiefs tattoos with more in the plans.

When Chiefs fans are mentioned around the world, many times my name and image come to their minds. In the last few years, though, I've realized that I made the Chiefs my idol. Now that's being replaced with God as my number one focus. I am learning that there is life outside of the Chiefs. This is the balance I've been needing for a really long time, as I cherish everything now.

I get to relax and take breaks from being XFactor, as I went way too hard for so many years. For a long time, my identity was XFactor and I forgot how to just be Ty. For a long time, due to addictions, I didn't love me. It wasn't until I started living a Christian life that I was able to love myself.

By not making the Chiefs my God, I've been able to focus on my loved ones and make time for them. As XFactor, I'm beyond unique, but now I don't try to be what others think I should be. I'm finally at peace being Ty who also plays the character of XFactor.

My passion has brought the Chiefs football into the lives of many people who weren't previously Chiefs fans.

"Put on the full armor of God, so that you can take
your stand against the devil's schemes."
Ephesians 6:11

CHAPTER 15

Superfan

I started dressing up in the early 1990s and, for seven years, I painted my body half red and yellow and wore a Chiefs wig, Chiefs shorts and Chiefs slippers. When Andre Rison came to town, he changed his nickname from Bad Moon A Rison to Spider man, and I took on that persona. Being Spider man made me a Superfan, and I got lost in all the attention. When Rison was cut, I vowed never to tie my persona to a player again, as I wanted something to last a lifetime. In 2000 when I created XFactor, that started to become a reality. In 2003 I flipped the script when Dante Hall took on that nickname because he hated being known as the Human Joystick.

Former Chiefs Player, Dante Hall, who got his nickname from me

In 30 years of being a Superfan, I've seen many dress up and ask me how to become a well-known fan. I try to give them advice, but many quit due to the negativity from others. After being on TV a few times, the luster goes away and fans struggle with finding purpose being a Superfan.

All the Superfans I know do charity work as their main reason, and they continue to do it year after year. Arrowman gave me advice when I first started dressing up. He said it won't be Raiders, Broncos, or Chargers fans that will say mean things about you, it will come from the Chiefs fans. Arrowman was right, as I've been to every opposing stadium except Atlanta. Sure, fans trash talk, but they never attack someone's character like I've experienced with Chiefs fans. My life was under a microscope and every word and action was questioned. With opposing fans, I take just as many pictures with them as Chiefs fans, but they respect the passion.

As a Superfan, I battled stereotypes of being a camera hog, attention seeker, and a drunk. I've made plenty of mistakes in my personal life. Fans get mad when the media gives me attention because they think my mistakes define me and are who I am. A lot of hate generates from jealousy of attention. A few will say I'm not a good role model; actually, it is my testimony to others of roads not to go down.

These factors discourage many dressed up fans from doing it for the long haul. I tell Superfans, "You have to be like a duck and let negative comments roll off you." I try to live with the 99% of fans who are positive. Having God to turn the negative stuff over to and to pray for the one casting stones has brought me peace. In the past, all those negative things said cut deeply and I had no place to release it. Now I try to be a positive person who loves everyone, just like Jesus.

I wish I had a dollar for every drunk fan that said, "XFactor retired, you need a new persona." For a long time, I would try to explain that I started XFactor in 2000, three years before Dante, but eventually I decided this was a waste of time. That one doesn't bother me anymore, as it's not my job to educate everyone and explain what I'm doing.

Everything now is magnified due to people knowing the XFactor image. I used to think as long as I did good things while in the XFactor outfit, what I did in my personal time was my own business. I found out the more exposure I received, the more those two personas were intertwined. I have owned up to my mistakes and seek to make amends to those I've hurt. Most of the mistakes happened when I was using alcohol and drugs, and all my legal problems were the result of my addiction. I struggled with how I could do a thousand good deeds for others, and no one would say anything, but with one mistake, the haters would share that on social media with everyone.

My haters also spread the most vicious rumors about me. Things like I stole money from charities (which was bold face lie). I donated more hours and dollars than I could count. In addition, they started rumors that I was a meth head even though I never used that drug. They also said I was a pedophile with child abuse in my background, which hurt because I have never done anything except love on kids, and adults were around every time.

These lies cut deep into my soul. So many people were influenced by the lies, and people trashed my name without knowing me. What hurt even more was that the lies were started by fans who wanted to destroy me so they could have more of the spotlight. Those I had introduced to charity work and helped make known became my worst enemies. I had good reasons for not involving them in my life and kicked a few of them out of my charity organization. What I couldn't understand was that all of them partied as hard as I did but didn't get into legal problems. It wasn't like I was being crucified by saints; maybe it was to deflect from their own flaws. It's sad that other fans can't support each other; it's a popularity contest. I viewed it as being on the same team and doing our part, not as a competition. Unfortunately, there are those that do.

Being XFactor, along with Arrowman and WeirdWolf, we were most known as Chiefs fans. With Arrowman being forced to quit due to Native American politics and WeirdWolf doing it part time over the last few years, that leaves me as the face of the fan base. Being in that position makes many want what I have. If that's what they want, they can have it. That isn't what motivates me. But it doesn't happen overnight and they have to build it just like we did. They crave the attention and jealousy drives them to try to destroy my image so they can take my place.

Being able to turn this over to God has removed all demons and hurt this brought into my life. I realized I can't make everyone happy; only those who are in my life daily. Studying Jesus's life and how he responded to those who persecuted him has given me a guide on how to deal with this. Anyone can hide behind a keyboard and say anything about someone on social media, but at the end of day, it doesn't matter, just as long as my loved ones know the truth. I can't spend time defending myself because it takes away from helping others. No matter what we do, we will have critics. Realizing our past doesn't define our future, we strive to be a better person than the day before. I'm blessed to have supporters who tell the truth and defend my name when others attack.

Who are you going to let be XFactor's in your life? I choose to be around positive people who build each other up versus those who tear others down. My haters are motivation to prove them wrong by living a Godly life. At the end of the day, it's not my job to judge them. That belongs to God. Every day I surrender to Jesus on my knees and ask for forgiveness of my sins. I let him rain his blood of mercy and grace into my life. That's who I want a relationship with more than anyone. If Jesus loves and approves of my life, that's all I need.

It's amazing to have apprentices under me that love God first. I can teach them God's ways to handle whatever the devil throws at them. The evil surrounding being a Superfan has ended the ride for thousands of fans across America. Being able to share my experiences with my new teammates helps steer them clear of pitfalls I fell into. I'll be the first to admit that the past Superfans I mentored, I failed because I was living in sin with them. I was a horrible teacher.

By doing it God's way now, my teammates and I can focus on doing things together minus any drama. By doing this, they will mentor other Superfans that come along and our legacy will be in them. If done right, a group of Superfans working as teammates can move mountains in communities across the Chiefs Kingdom. All glory goes to God by doing good works in and through us.

There will always be two types of Superfans: the selfish ones who want popularity and the ones who want to use their platform to help others. When I started dressing up, I did it to get on TV so my family, especially my dad, could see me. I'm beyond thankful, grateful, and blessed that God used it to help so many. I honestly think everyone starts dressing up to get more attention. The ones across America who end up doing it for decades by helping others are a common denominator. If it didn't happen to me, I would have given it up many years ago. I think that's why so many quit. Negativity outweighs the attention. I'm powered by smiles and happiness. It is XFactor that keeps me putting on the outfit and going to battle, year after year.

"And those who belong to Christ Jesus have crucified
the flesh with its passions and desires."
Galatians 5:24

"To the weak I became weak, that I might win the weak.
I have become all things to all people, that
by all means I might save some."
1 Corinthians 9:22

"There is no fear in love, but perfect love casts out fear.
For fear has to do with punishment, and whoever fears
has not been perfected in love."
1 John 4:18

CHAPTER 16

Being XFactor to Others

Whether we are a positive influence or a negative influence, we are an XFactor to every person we meet. A simple smile and hello to a stranger can change their whole day. A simple question of "How you are doing?" or a message of "I was thinking about you," can let them know they are not alone. The devil wants us to live in fear, worry and depression. He wants our world to be in complete darkness. By being a light to others, God brings light into the world.

Having over 200,000 social media followers, I see the impact that posts can have on others either positively or negatively. I found that drama excites others, they love living in negativity because it makes them feel better about their lives. It is human nature to get caught up in chaos. Followers are easily influenced by what people say and tend to go with the majority, even if it's wrong. Those who follow negativity lack confidence and seek approval from others. This doesn't allow them to let God shine in their lives.

On the flip side, inspiring posts can empower people to do positive things for others. Fewer people are true leaders who don't care as much what others think but instead let God shine through them. I've known both sides of being a leader by either leading them into destructive ways or by influencing them to do good for others. I'm grateful that God is casting out the ways the devil influenced me. Now I have the Holy Spirit leading me as a light to others.

God allows choice. What type of XFactor do you want to be toward others? Someone who destroys or someone who builds them up? God gives us our own platforms to influence those in our lives. The million-dollar question is, are we going to bring fire into their lives or be living water for them?

When I allowed the devil into my life, so much destruction happened that directly impacted everyone around me. The devil told me I was only hurting myself, but I discovered that to be biggest lie, as I caused worry and pain into my loved one's lives. When we suffer, others will take on our suffering because they love us so much. Others will validate and hide their flaws by pointing at our mistakes.

I've learned that praying for those who want me to fail is the most powerful thing we can do. Showing compassion and love to those casting stones takes away any evil power they have over me. Jesus showed us the way to do this in the Bible, *"Forgive them Father as they don't know what they are doing"* Luke 23:34.

By living this way, maybe they will look in the mirror and want to treat others better. Maybe they won't, but at least we fight fire with water and not with more fire. On the flip side, by living like God, we show, through action, how we can overcome anything. It takes away suffering, which also takes away the suffering and worrying of our loved ones.

To our families, friends, coworkers and strangers, we don't realize how big an XFactor we are or could be to them. We are influenced by the people we surround ourselves with. There were times in my life where I was beyond miserable. Looking back, it was the product of me and people I surrounded myself with.

We typically spend the majority of time with people we have things in common with. I've seen both extremes: hanging with addicts and hanging with Christians. When I have been around positive people, mountains have been moved. Some have taught me hard lessons and others have inspired me more than words. I'm not afraid of XFactor's who are struggling if they are seeking to change for the better. Being completely broken before, I can relate to those broken and offer ways to find victory through our Savior. Not everyone is at the same point as me and they don't want to change. That's when we simply pray for them.

Sports taught me that there is no "I" in team. Sports taught me the power of having teammates. The power of a team working together can do unbelievable things. A team can also destroy others' lives if their motives are twisted. By joining team God, we can overcome anything evil principalities throw at us. I now wear the XFactor outfit because I want it to stand for God, my greatest XFactor. By living in God's will and not mine, I celebrate Super Bowl type victories every day. Forever I was on the devil's team. It wasn't fun being on a losing team. How amazing the world would be if we all loved each other just like God loves us! Our differences make us unique in the ways God made each one of us. What if we embraced our differences instead of fighting them? Hopefully my words will inspire you to look at yourself and ask the question, "What kind of XFactor am I to others?" Maybe challenge yourself to change and improve so that you are showing others God's love.

Writing this book made me look inward to see how I was treating others. It helped me grow and is backed by God's Word in the Bible on how to treat everyone. My prayer is that through my struggles, my words that come from God, can help someone who is lost as I once was. My prayers are that you can grow to be a positive XFactor to those you come in contact with. I hope your dreams stay big and your worries stay small.

"Your word is a lamp to my feet and a light to my path."
Psalm 119:105

"And those who are wise shall shine like the brightness of the sky above;
and those who turn many to righteousness, like the stars forever and ever."
Daniel 12:3

"Arise, shine; for your light has come, And the
glory of the LORD has risen upon you."
Isaiah 60:1

CHAPTER 17

Ty and XFactor

No matter where I travel, I meet new Chiefs fans, especially at road games. So many haven't experienced Arrowhead stadium due to where they live, and I see how impactful me being on TV all these years has been, as they are excited to meet me.

I have friends who call and say, "I'm with people who don't believe we are best friends." Through this conversation I get a glimpse of how big the XFactor image is. Where I struggle is putting Ty before XFactor. My self-worth was that I was XFactor and didn't allow people to get to know the real Ty. I chased fame because I thought that's what my purpose was. I didn't like Ty and tried to put on the image as XFactor being popular to help hide my flaws. God has allowed me to love Ty and realize that it is Ty who makes XFactor, not XFactor who makes Ty.

For years my friends have told me, "I know Ty. Everyone else just knows XFactor." They loved Ty first. Sure, they thought the XFactor stuff was cool, but that wasn't the reason they wanted to be part of my life. In my biggest struggles, it was these friends who rose to help me. Some of the others who just knew XFactor tried to destroy me or were silent.

Forever fame had me putting XFactor as my God, which was my self-will. My life wasn't transformed until I surrendered completely to Jesus. God always wanted me to seek Him first and have a relationship with Him. God's blessings are more powerful that any I received on my own. When I made the decision to put Ty first and seek God first, my life changed for the better. Being Ty, a Child of God, is more rewarding than being a man full of pride, which XFactor caused. Learning to love myself, with God's help, has allowed me to love everyone. I had to experience knowing that God's love for me was always the same. God loves me the exact same when I fail as when I have victories. Feeling His love allowed me to love myself.

Chasing fame was a never-ending battle and I was never fulfilled, no matter what things happened. True happiness has come from stepping outside that world and loving the blessings God has placed in my life, even the smallest ones. A peace has come over me that has emerged through God's mercy, grace and love. Humility has risen where pride reigned through surrendering completely to God's will and not my own.

I'm an ordinary man thrust into extraordinary circumstances. The road I used to be on was certain death, now that road is eternal life. I used to worry about death, but now it doesn't scare me, because I know that will actually be the greatest day of my life. I'll be able to go to Heaven for eternity and live in all of God's splendor.

The biggest struggle with those who experience fame is knowing how to deal with it. It is easy to forget who you are. I was lost from who I was in my soul. I'm thankful God brought me this storm and revealed who I truly am. Many people turn to alcohol and drugs to escape the reality fame brings and they end up dying. I'm one of the fortunate few to make it through and am now writing about it.

Often, I wonder, "Why me, God? I have not been worthy to deserve this." I realized that God will be glorified by the works He performs in me. Having so many die from this motivated me to seek God with my heart so that I didn't end up being another statistic. I'm thankful, grateful, and blessed that God put XFactor's in my life that He speaks through to open my eyes. Having thousands of people pray for me during my toughest times saved my life. As God answered them and spared my life, so I can hopefully lead others to Him.

Where XFactor was the biggest influence on my life, now God is my number one focus. I have learned that XFactor was a gift from God that allows me a bigger platform to share how amazing He is.

"The world and its desires pass away,
but whoever does the will of God lives forever."
1 John 2:17

"For all that is in the world—the desires of the flesh,
the desires of the eyes, and the pride of life—is not
from the Father but from the world."
1 John 2:16

CHAPTER 18

Living Two Different Lives

As I reflect on my life, I realize there are two different sides. The sober periods where God worked in me and periods where chemicals from the devil ran my life. I was sober from 2007-2010, from 2012-2017, and now sober since July 30, 2017.

In those times of being sober, I've been the greatest XFactor to others. I became addicted to helping others rather than chemicals. Two charity organizations arose, three Guinness World records fell, and so many lives were impacted by me and my teammates. My relationships with friends and family were also restored during those periods. My heart swells with love for others when I'm sober. I'm honest on social media and in life about my struggles. This vulnerability allows others to come to me for help when they struggle.

When using drugs and alcohol, I was just going down the same road to destruction with others. In sobriety, my story can give hope to those struggling in the same battlefronts I had. I share my story in hopes of planting a seed of going from ashes to growing into a tree that bears fruit. Through forgiveness of Jesus, I share everything without shame. Sober Ty living for God and the man consumed by the devil's poison is night and day different. I was a monster when I was using drugs and alcohol, caring only about myself. Living sober through God, passion reigns to love and help everyone. Having a huge platform to share how God has changed a wretch like me into one who lives in His glory is amazing. Can one person make a difference in the lives of others? I believe I can because of what God has done for me.

God has given us all gifts to be able to help others. Being the one lost sheep in wilderness, being devoured by wolves from the devil, allows me to be on the level of others when they are lost. Being a sober child of God, a humble, kind, caring, and loving man has emerged from the monster I once was. I know only God can change the world so that isn't my job, but I can share the Good Word with others. Peace comes from knowing this. I just need to play my part by allowing God to work through me.

His will reigns in my life when I'm sober and seeking Him. I've seen the other side, and its darkness consumed me. By placing chemicals and my will as my god, a monster was the result. I did things I would never do with God and sobriety in my life. I lived in a world of fear, doubt, worrying, and ultimate pain in addiction. I was numb to my feelings by the chemicals I abused. I felt alone and different than anyone else in addiction. I'm thankful for the consequences of being in jail because it humbled me and turned my heart toward seeking God.

Sometimes I wonder what I could have accomplished had I stayed sober my entire life. Then I realize I had to go through my sins to truly have a testimony and glorify God. It's amazing how God allowed me to go through every storm but still put a hedge of protection around me. I needed to experience every storm so I could grow and be where God needed me. That's how my faith was strengthened. God brought me through the toughest storms imaginable. It was like living in hell on Earth, being chained down by the devil, whose chains always held me back from living in God's glory and finding happiness.

I was a negative XFactor to many people in my world. Now I can share how God is the biggest XFactor in my life, which trickles down to the relationships I have with others. Each day I grow farther from the monster I was when I was rolling with the devil, and more toward living a Christlike life. Living in the fruits of the spirit is the most amazing feeling I've had in my life. Everything the devil offered was the exact opposite of the fruits of the spirit. But going down that opposite road allows me to cherish everything God has to offer.

"The thief approaches with malicious intent, looking to steal, slaughter, and destroy; I came to give life with joy and abundance."
John 10:10

"Before I formed you in the womb I knew you, before you were born I set you apart; I appointed you as a prophet to the nations."
Jeremiah 1:5

CHAPTER 19

Daily Life

So many people are curious about my daily life when I'm not being XFactor. Unfortunately, in society, most people are defined by their career. I've never been made that way; I love to put in a hard day's work, but I'm not defined by the job I'm doing. A lot of people think that XFactor is my job, but it's just a hobby. I pay full price for my tickets just like an ordinary fan, even though many say I should get in for free.

I met with the Chiefs management team many years ago and we made a mutual agreement that I wouldn't go the "getting compensated" route. If I had been compensated, I would be owned by the NFL and have to get approval for everything I do. I chose freedom to attend any event and do whatever I wanted with all other organizations.

To make money to support my activities, I worked at handicapped facilities for 14 years. I then ran tool repair for the Midwest hub for Fastenal. I've been a Medicare insurance salesman, farmer, construction worker, print press operator, and automotive salesman. Once in a while, I made commercials or national promotions.

I have a beautiful angel daughter and a son. I didn't know I was father to a son for 17 years. He was conceived during my wild college days. I thought he was my roommate's kid and was told the baby was given up for adoption. His mom found me on Facebook as a friend of one of her childhood friends. The stepfather who raised my son reached out to me and offered to pay for a DNA test.

The first time I met my son, I knew he was mine. I was shocked to find out that I had been a dad for 17 years. I always wanted a boy to carry on my legacy, and God blessed me 17 years before I knew it. I wish our relationship was stronger but it's difficult since he is growing into a man and world is crazy. But as we get older, God will grow our relationship.

My daily life, especially during football season, is busy and crazy. Having over 200,000 social media followers is like having a full-time job. I don't want to be like other celebrities who never respond to comments or messages, so I make sure to answer them all. I want to be available to others, especially if I can help.

My friends joke and say, "When it comes to the Chiefs, fans use you more than Google for information." I actually love passing on my knowledge and helping fans. On gamedays, friends like walking around the parking lot with me to meet all the fans and to see all the things Arrowhead has to offer. I only stop for a few minutes at tailgates, as I need to touch and fire up the fans. I'm usually at the stadium for 12-13 hours so I can see as many fans as possible.

Everywhere I go, I experience blessings as I get love from fans all over the world. I love taking pictures with fans, as it gives me the opportunity to learn where they are from. Their excitement of meeting me fires me up more and more throughout the day. Using the porta potty is the only time I'm not interacting with fans, but many times they stand outside and talk to me.

In Arrowhead, it's my job to get fans to stand and scream, so I am constantly waving my arms up and down to signal this. Then I crash as soon as I get home because it requires every bit of energy to energize others.

Forever in public, I would wear Chiefs from head to toe, which allowed fans to recognize me. I enjoyed interactions with these fans, but I've recently toned it down so I can be normal once in a while. As soon as one person recognizes me and says, "XFactor," then everyone comes around. I love this, but it is tough to get basic errands done on my time off.

Every girl I have dated eventually gets tired of all the attention I get. They will say, "We can't go anywhere and have alone time." I personally love it, but it causes jealousy; maybe that's the reason I have never been married. I have to budget time and leave 30 minutes early so I have time to interact with fans.

Not blending into society allows me time to meet some amazing people. But I also need time to figure out how to help the community. Every chance away from attention, I go to a lake. This is where I can be alone and spend time with God in His greatest creations. This is where I find complete and total peace to unwind from the chaos that is my abnormal life. I love the challenge of trying to find the fish and seeing what they are biting on. It's the only place I will shut off my phone and disconnect from the world. I also enjoy joining a few friends for a round of golf. I do these activities to achieve serenity.

Long gone are the days of partying around the clock. Those days have been replaced by church, AA, and NA meetings. Church is where my true growth and healing happen. I go as often as I can. In KC, I'm blessed to find a service almost every day of the week.

I'm finding time for my friends and loved ones as I sacrificed that in the past. With older age, I've learned to slow down instead of living each day like it is my last. For a long time, I tried to live a legendary life where everyone would know and remember me. Now I don't care about my legacy, only that everyone has the opportunity to know Jesus.

I cherish time with people who love me versus entertaining the masses. Many friends have nicknamed me Superman, which is a good description. As Ty, I'm quiet and relaxed, but as soon as I put on the XFactor outfit, I become a different person. It's like holding back energy as Ty and then exploding as XFactor. My personality is more exciting than Clark Kent though, as I love to joke around and act like a big kid. For a long time, I was able to hide behind my costume, especially when it came to speaking in front of others. Growing up, I was petrified of doing this; now I'm comfortable speaking in public. Through God, I've been able to be Ty who also plays the character of XFactor.

God has become the number one focus of my daily life. I pray every day, and almost everything I watch or listen to centers around God. For many years God was nonexistent to me; now my life is consumed with Him. Victory is happening where defeat has been. I tell people, "God made me an ordinary man thrown into extraordinary circumstances."

I'm rarely a follower of the crowds but love trailblazing into new wildernesses. By living for God, I can lead others in a more impactful way. Many look at my life differently. Many gain inspiration from the way I face my flaws and how God is removing them. For a long time, I didn't think people saw me as a role model or inspiration, so I didn't care. But seeing that my life does help others, I want to live more Christlike.

Everyday I'm blessed to have positive XFactor's in my life who pray for me, support me, and help me when I struggle. Sometimes our circles must become much smaller to find the power in them. Most years I come in contact with at least a million people. It's difficult to figure out who is with me or who is out to hurt me. I've struggled with the question, "Do people care about me or do they just care about what I can get them?"

Through my biggest storms, God answered that question. People will show their true colors when we suffer. Either they will help us dig out of the hole or throw more dirt on top of us. When I struggled, I had to unfriend and block a couple thousand followers on social media, but that's okay; I only want friends who are positive influences on each other. Especially on Facebook. This is a constant windmill, as I always have thousands who become my friend to replace the ones I blocked. As my circle gets smaller, I find out who truly loves me, and that's where strength lies.

We are all XFactor's to each other. The million-dollar question is, "Are you a positive or negative influence on each other?"

"For he chose us in him before the creation of the world to be holy
and blameless in his sight. In love he predestined us for adoption
to sonship through Jesus Christ, in accordance with his pleasure and will."
Ephesians 1:4

"Nevertheless, the firm foundation of God stands, having this seal,
'The Lord knows those who are His,' and,
'Everyone who names the name of the Lord
is to abstain from wickedness.'"
1 Timothy 2:19

CHAPTER 20

Javon Belcher Story

I first met Javon Belcher in River Falls, Wisconsin at the Chiefs Training Camp. I asked coach Herm Edwards, "Who is the camp star?" He answered, "Number 59, Javon Belcher." When I talked to Javon the next day, I told him what the coach said. He responded, "Don't tell me that. It puts extra pressure on me."

Javon was an undrafted player that year. He and I became close, especially with his mom. She sat in my section at Arrowhead Stadium and was at the players parking lot when I took kids there to meet the players. The second game of the year, he hurt his shoulder and they put him on strong narcotics. His mom would update me every home game about the situation. She told me he couldn't go on the injured list because his linebacker coach would scream and tell him they would replace him.

Javon also had pressures coming from the baby momma who was carrying his first kid. She was threatening to leave Javon and take the baby, which would leave Javon to pay a huge child support. Fellow teammate, Jamal Charles, introduced Javon to his girlfriend through the woman he was dating. He made a small salary but had signed for a minimum of 1.5 million. His mom was concerned about the situation.

Fast forward … the Chiefs tried getting them both into counseling, but she wouldn't go. Pressure started getting to Javon, but, as a middle linebacker, he was supposed to be the strong one. I sent a message to Javon a week before letting him know that I was concerned about his baby momma situation. I was going through similar things with my baby momma and wanted to talk to him. He responded, "I love you man. Continue to rock the Chiefs Kingdom. Go Chiefs!" Javon and I both had trouble asking for help.

Fast forward to the night before the shootings. Javan was probably on pain killers and was confirmed to be drinking. The cops talked to him at his new girlfriend's house. He slept on her couch till he sobered up and then drove to his house in Independence, Missouri where his baby momma was. A fight ensued and he shot the baby momma. His mom ran in and he hugged and kissed her. With tears in his eyes, he said, "I have to go."

Javon then drove to Arrowhead Stadium as cop cars went to his house. He called the Chiefs office and asked for Coach Gibbs, Coach Romel Crennel, and GM Scott Pioli to meet him. He was kneeling and praying when the coaches found him. Then he raised a pistol to his temple as the cop car sirens headed in his direction. Javon had gone too far to ever come back. The thought of being incarcerated for the rest of his life was too much to bear; he pulled the trigger.

I regret that I was not able to talk to him and offer support. I missed my friend for a long time. Going to the game the next week at Arrowhead Stadium, I cried most of the game.

Hug your loved ones and talk to them; you never know when they will leave this earth.

CHAPTER 21

Raiders/Chiefs

Being inducted into the Pro Football Hall of Fame allowed me an opportunity to meet the best Superfans across America. Historically the Chiefs and Raiders have been one of the most bitter rivalries. This is also true when it comes to the fans; hatred prevails between the two fan bases.

At Canton, Ohio when I was inducted, I met Raider Ron who they called the General. Our differences drew us together with friendly trash talking. We discovered we were similar in all ways except for the teams we represented. Working together with a charity event that benefited the United Way in Canton, we realized our hearts were similar. We became brothers from day one. Society said we were supposed to hate each other, so we talked about what we could do to change that. Maybe we could make social media posts showing the most recognizable fans coming together and that would trickle down to other fans.

For the previous 18 years, Raider Ron had not missed a Raiders game, either home or away. He attended over 290 straight games. I have attended 100 away games over the past 25 years, but Ron did 145 away games in 18 years. His dedication in traveling to games blows me away.

After meeting Ron in Canton, I spent time with him every time the Raiders played at Arrowhead. He was XFactor in my life because he was one of the original Superfans and I learned from his experiences. He tried to get Arrowman and me to come to Oakland. For years, we said, "No thanks. We want to live." The stereotype was that Raiders fans would hurt opposing fans if they entered the Black Hole. Finally in 2013, I told Ron, "Okay, I'll put my life in your hands." I had about 50 friends who said they would go with me. But as the time got closer, they backed out. I called Ron and said, "I'm going to cancel my trip because nobody wants to come with me." He promised, "I will protect you and not let anyone hurt you." Raider Ron and three other Superfans picked me up at the airport. They were excited that I was doing this unprecedented thing. That weekend, the love between me and Ron grew to a new level. I learned to trust a man who was supposed to be my enemy. I got roasted by every Raiders fan, but it wasn't in a mean way. I was told they respected what I stood for, and Ron was the first to tell them about my charity work.

Having Ron endorse me was powerful, and the Chiefs / Raiders rivalry became my favorite game experience. At Arrowhead I experience ultimate love. This was the opposite, but underneath there was love among us Superfans. I was on National TV during the game which was a powerful image to Chiefs fans across the world. Many said, "Wow, XFactor is the craziest Chiefs fan for going into the Black Hole." The pictures we took were posted on social media so the world could see that we love each other.

On that trip, my relationship with Violator, the most recognized Raider's fan, grew. The next 3 years, I took other Chiefs Superfans to Oakland to experience what I talked about. When I decided to create my National Charity organization, Raider Ron and Violator were the first people I called. It was great to work together on something we had talked about and dreamed of doing.

Early on it was clear that Raider Ron's health was fading. Even though I knew he was in extreme pain, his passion for this project was unmatched. What if we could bring fan bases together to do charity work? This would go a long way toward defeating hatred across all fan bases.

It was a tough day when I received a call that Raider Ron had grown his angel wings. Through our friendship, we called each other "brother" and always said, "I love you." Never would I have imagined that one of my best friends would be a Raiders fan.

Ron was the XFactor who introduced me to Raider Nation and orchestrated me becoming friends with other Superfans, especially Violator. When I relapsed, our dream of Legends of the Stands came crashing down. Violator has replaced Raider Ron as one of my best friends. We still talk about making this a reality of bringing fan bases together and teaming up for charity work.

Even though we aren't doing big activities together, we talk a lot. Violator gives glory to God in everything, and we are brothers in Christ. We talk about how the world says we should not be friends because I am white, he is an African American, I'm a Chiefs fan and he's a Raiders fan. He helps me when I'm attacked by other fans and he gives me great advice. Few in my circle can relate to what I go through. Violator, as the most recognizable Raider's fan, has experienced the things I have as XFactor. It's amazing to have a friend I can turn to for help or advice.

My relationship with the Raiders Superfans showed me that no matter what the differences, if we give people an opportunity, they can be a blessing. The world is divided today, and we can learn a lot from these relationships, especially between Violator and me. All we have to do is open our heart and not follow what society says.

*"But I say unto you, Love your enemies, bless them that curse you,
do good to them that hate you, and pray for them which
despitefully use you, and persecute you."*
Matthew 5:44

*"But I say unto you which hear, Love your enemies,
do good to them which hate you."*
Luke 6:27

*"Beloved, let us love one another: for love is of God;
and every one that loveth is born of God, and knoweth God."*
1 John 4:7 KJV

CHAPTER 22

Patrick Mahomes and Players

Each year, the NFL draft is one of my favorite events. I started going to draft parties at Arrowhead Stadium over 20 years ago. Dressing as a Superfan, reporters wanted to interview me about who I wanted our Chiefs to pick, so I started studying the college players. On many occasions, we drafted players I said we would draft in the first round. I called the shot with Derrick Johnson, Dwayne Bowe, Eric Berry, and Glen Dorsey on local medias.

In 2003 I started taking angels with me to the draft day experience. These kids enjoyed it more than most fans; they never had an experience like it. In 2017 I took 10 angels. I studied the players and was aware that we needed a strong-armed quarterback. I loved Alex Smith, but he didn't have the arm for our speedy wide receivers.

Patrick Mahomes had the "IT" factor. He was a hardworking, humble kid with gifts like no other QB. Upon arriving at Arrowhead, my angels asked me who we would be drafting and I told them, "Patrick Mahomes." Three local news stations interviewed me asking who XFactor thought we would choose. I answered, "We will trade up and select Patrick Mahomes from Texas Tech." All three reporters thought I was crazy and said we had more pressing needs. They said, "If we take a QB, it will be Deshaun

Watson. He's a more proven QB." I answered, "We can continue to be satisfied with just going to the playoffs, or we can make a move like this and win a Super Bowl. Watson will be a good QB, but Mahomes will be a superstar."

When Mitch Holthaus came to the stage to announce the Chiefs had traded with Buffalo for the 10th pick, I knew who they were taking, even though the fans were screaming "Watson." After the pick was announced, "Patrick Mahomes," all three reporters bowed toward me. Later they told me I was the only person they interviewed who had called the shot. My friends, angels, and angel's parents couldn't believe what happened.

God puts so many things on my heart about Patrick Mahomes. Patrick is also a child of God who gives all glory to God. Going into our Super Bowl year at training camp, God put heavy on my heart that Patrick was going to get hurt that season, but we would be all right. Peace came over me. When Patrick was hurt in Denver, I knew God would miraculously heal him. God had seen me through enormous storms and more blessings than I could imagine were on the other side. The same thing happened to our Chiefs. We won the Super Bowl for the first time in 50 years. The year I put God first instead of the Chiefs was the year we won the championship I had dreamed of.

Our owner, Clark Hunt, Patrick, and many other players gave God credit first, which made my heart full of love. God had a hand in helping us overcome the biggest deficits and challenges that year. During that year, I decided to have "Patrick" tattooed on my forearm. That's how much I believe and love the kid the world said would never become an elite NFL QB. What do experts know? God placed on my heart what would happen if we took that amazing Texas kid.

"So do not fear, for I am with you;
do not be dismayed, for I am your God.
I will strengthen you and help you;
I will uphold you with my righteous right hand."
Isaiah 41:10

"But those who hope in the Lord
will renew their strength.
They will soar on wings like eagles;
they will run and not grow weary,
they will walk and not be faint."
Isaiah 40:31

Players

When a player is cut, traded, or retires, it's sad for the Chiefs fans. It hurts me because of my personal connection with them, but it doesn't end because they're no longer playing for the Chiefs. Players tell me that life after football is tough because they go from being loved to being forgotten. I can relate; I used to struggle every year when the season was over. In the early years, I would go from everyone knowing me as XFactor to nobody knowing me as Ty. That's when my charity organization emerged, allowing XFactor to be visible throughout the year.

Now my friendship with the players grows because I never forget them and I ask them to help me with my charity work. In my younger days, I would party with the players, and I saw different sides of players who needed to escape from the pressures of fame. As I've gotten older, I started doing charity events with many of the players. I saw firsthand how amazing their hearts are. When autographing an item for me, they ask, "Which charity is this going to, X?" They love contributing to great causes.

As the popularity of XFactor increased, players would tell me how much it meant to play for me. They would share that in college, they had seen me on TV getting the fans worked up. When the players come back to Arrowhead after they leave, they find me and tell me how much they missed me. Our bond is cemented during their time with the Chiefs and never goes away, as we are always family. Few fans have their heroes becoming their friends. I'm blessed to see a side of players very few see.

The Chiefs are the biggest XFactor in the sports world to bring us together as family. I'm also blessed to know a lot of the players' families. It touches my heart when the player's kids want a picture with me, and they love playing with me, as I am the biggest kid. One thing that I realized is this: the players are just ordinary people like me thrown into extraordinary situations.

"My flesh and my heart may fail,
but God is the strength of my heart
and my portion forever."
Psalm 73:26

"I love you, Lord, my strength.
The Lord is my rock, my fortress and my deliverer;
my God is my rock, in whom I take refuge,
my shield and the horn of my salvation, my stronghold."
Psalm 18:1-2

CHAPTER 23

Media

Over the years I have been on the cover of Sports Illustrated Football Edition, Sporting News, and have been in articles for Maxim, Playboy and other magazines. I've been on National TV during almost every game during the last 20 plus years. ESPN and NFL Network and many local news stations use clips of me when talking about the Chiefs. About every newspaper in America has featured me in an article, especially when I've done interviews with Associated Press. I've done more interviews with local media than I can count, and I've been on hundreds of radio stations across the country. Also, social media sites use my image whenever they do articles related to the Chiefs.

Sports Illustrated 2012 Edition. I'm on the bottom row.

For many years I was excited by the exposure. Over the years, though, my excitement grew because my loved ones would get excited by it. One year Man vs Food put me on their Super Bowl special for about 10 minutes. When National TV puts me on during games, my phone vibrates from fans all over the world.

Today I view media exposure as an opportunity to glorify God and call attention to the causes I'm supporting. When someone requests an interview, I try to steer the questions toward charity and God. The media is a great tool that allows me to move mountains in communities, but a 15-minute interview for TV can be edited down to their agenda. Some media will edit what I say to short clips, so it conveys what they want, not what I actually said.

For the most part, especially Kansas City, media does an amazing job of highlighting what I want to get out. I try to spin positive thoughts, even on negative stories. Something I'm proud of is that I've never bashed the Chiefs organization, fans, or players. Unfortunately, when it comes to controversial subjects, this costs me airtime as the media's ratings are more important to them and negativity gets the highest ratings. This is a huge problem with society today as we believe whatever media feeds us.

I respect the privacy of players, but I also know what goes on behind the scenes. An example is that Willie Roaf told me he was retiring a month before he announced it to the media. When players tell me things confidently, I don't tell anyone. This is why I have close relationships with players.

By being on all types of media, I have the opportunity to meet new fans. XFactor has become someone that fans from all over the world want to meet and get pictures with. I'll never know the full impact of my image being used by media, but all experiences with fans gives me a glimpse of the magnitude it has.

It's mind-boggling to think that during certain games as many as 50 million people see me. Growing up in a small town of 3,000, these numbers are hard to comprehend, but my actions should always reflect my walk with Christ, and I try to walk and live like Jesus did. I fail daily but I'm growing and being pruned in His direction, and He is transforming me. I once struggled for wanting to be "famous" and seeking validation through media. Now I want all glory to go to God. I've been humbled in this area by God's grace and mercy.

*"But the Lord is faithful, and he will strengthen
you and protect you from the evil one."*
2 Thessalonians 3:3

*"He gives strength to the weary
and increases the power of the weak."*
Isaiah 40:29

CHAPTER 24

Alone

There is a saying, "It's lonely on top." For a long time, I struggled with who to talk to about my problems. My loved ones couldn't relate to things I experienced.

Being XFactor, I was in a place where pressure to be a role model and my addictions clashed. When I made a mistake, I was judged by those who had no idea what I was going through. I struggled with not wanting to burden others with my problems, thinking I could fight through them. My escape was to get loaded, numb the pain, and keep busy so I wouldn't have to think about the mess I had made.

The Javon Belcher tragedy opened my eyes to how I bottled things up. I had reached out to Javon a week before the tragedy, and his response to my message was, "I love you, brother. Go Chiefs!" He put on a strong front like I did instead of confiding in someone about what was going on. I thought my image needed to be one of control, which was the furthest from the truth. I didn't like negativity so I wouldn't talk about the bad things. Just like Javon, others saw signs that something was wrong, but when they asked, "Are you all right?" my answer was, "I'm superfantabulous. I'm living the dream."

Actually, I was living a nightmare. I had two lives – the one I wanted the world to see and the one I tried to keep a secret. I was ashamed of the man I was behind the scenes – one who was broken and depressed. I tried to become more famous and wore myself out by doing every charity activity I could. That way, others would not see my flaws but would praise the good work I was doing. This battle eventually broke me. In AA and NA, I found people I could talk to with similar struggles. I still had things they could not relate to when it came to pressures of fame.

When I was at my lowest, I had two XFactors rise who are former Chiefs players. The first call was from former Chiefs kicker, Nick Lowery. He called me at 2 a.m. from San Diego because he saw me in desperate need of help. The things he told me about fame opened my eyes. He said, "I could make 30 field goals in a row and be loved by everyone. But if I missed one field goal, even if I had an injury or weather elements were horrible, then everyone hated me." I could relate to this. I did thousands of good deeds, but as soon as I made one mistake, none of that mattered. This was the constant battle I dealt with. Nick also talked about when he went to the Jets, how everyone in KC abandoned him. I felt the same way – how could everyone abandon me when I made one mistake? Nick was my childhood hero, and he was taking the time to help me moved me. Finally, I had someone who could relate to what I was dealing with.

Shortly after that, Louis Aguiar, the Chiefs former punter, called. Even when he was in New York as a coach, we had stayed in contact. He relayed his experiences and struggles with fame, and we talked regularly. His advice helped me beyond words!

Nick and Louie were enormous XFactor's, helping me understand what was going on in my crazy life. This had been missing. By working together, they helped turn a struggle into a strength within me. These relationships have only grown stronger through our brokenness. Now I understand the power of a simple phone call when we are struggling.

With all I've done, I can usually relate to those who are lost; a place I know very well. Being able to relate and offer advice on how I handled situations can give hope to others.

Also during this time, God placed a third XFactor in my life. My superfan teammate Steve "The Owner" Tate from the Packers reached out. Steve has over 30 years of sobriety. His advice helped me with both addiction and fame. Steve knew the pressures and temptations of being a well-known Superfan. How he dealt with it was beyond inspirational, and he had the balance I desired. It was evident that God was the One he relied on in every area of his life.

These three XFactor's were puzzle pieces I needed who all pointed me toward Jesus. It's amazing how God brings people into our life when we need them the most. My life has been transformed by God. He placed people in my life from church, AA, family, and friends. All these puzzle pieces are essential to assist me from moving away from the monster I once was. I allowed negative XFactor's into my life and suffered because of it. By replacing them with positive XFactor's, I have been completely transformed.

"Then the LORD God said, 'It is not good for the man to be alone. I will make a helper who is just right for him.'"
Genesis 2:18

"I am crucified with Christ: nevertheless I live; yet not I, but Christ liveth in me: and the life which I now live in the flesh I live by the faith of the Son of God, who loved me, and gave himself for me."
Galatians 2:20 KJV

"Don't be afraid, because I'm with you; don't be anxious,
because I am your God. I keep on strengthening
you; I'm truly helping you.
I'm surely upholding you with my victorious right hand."
Isaiah 41:10

CHAPTER 25

Spiritual Warfare #1

I relapsed on my birthday May 8th, 2017, after being clean and sober for five years. I told God that day that I didn't believe in Him if He could take innocent angels and leave a wretch like me on Earth. I had received a call at 12:04 a.m. that my angel Aimee had passed away. This was 6th young angel to die in just a year. I couldn't understand God's plan in all this. Why did He take perfectly innocent, beautiful kids and leave a sinner like me on Earth. I would have gladly died instead if one of my angels would have a long fulfilling life in my place. I didn't believe in God anymore which sent me spiraling out of control.

Without God in my life leading the way, the devil had complete control. I had a couple of projects I was working on that took over all my focus. I had been saving money for years to open a sports store like old SportsNutz by the stadiums. This was going to be my daughter's store, which she would eventually run when she got older. She was beyond happy when I took her to the new store. She even helped write the check for the first 3 months' rent. I became obsessed with making her dreams come true.

At first, I got a smart business partner, but my reckless ways caused by my drinking quickly ended that business relationship. That was the first sign that this may not work, but I was so consumed in self-will that I charged forward. I had so many friends who wanted to see this store become a reality. Many of them came to the store and helped me transform it. I was making horrible business decisions and went crazy on my spending, and I started partying when I wasn't at the store. To cover all the pain I felt, I turned to all demons from the past with alcohol and drugs.

Another business partner came into the picture which gave me hope that we could get this done. He was also an alcoholic, and we quickly fell into the "working hard and partying harder" lifestyle. In addition, I had big Hollywood companies interested in a reality show featuring stores and National Superfan buddies that I had teamed up with. The devil consumed me with greed as he said, "Soon you will be making more money than you could ever imagine." I thought that lots of money would cure everything broken in me and in my world.

In the beginning, I wanted a store so I could fund all my charity dreams. But instead of investing all my money in dreams, I started dating a couple of strippers and spending all my money on them, plus chemicals. I loaned my back-up car to a dancer I was dating. After a month, I started having mechanical issues with my main vehicle and I asked her to bring my car back. She always had excuses or would ignore my calls. Finally, I told her if I didn't get it back that night, I would call the cops and report it stolen. Later that night, she called and said the car had been stolen but not to worry because she had called the cops. I called St. Joseph Law Enforcement and started working with them to find my vehicle. After many hours, I received a call from a cop. He said, "I have good news and bad news. The good news is that we've recovered your car; the bad news is that it was used in two robberies. A liquor store and a convenience store. The four African Americans ran into a rival gang member and drug dealer who was walking down the street. The individuals in the car opened fire on him, hitting him in the chest

3 times. He, in return, fired 7 shots back into the car. Shortly after, the cops found the car and attempted to pull them over. The suspects traveled up to 145 mph on a donut tire. After 15 miles the tire blew out and we apprehended them. The bad news is this: the man who was shot 3 times passed away, so your car needs to be impounded for a month while we conduct an investigation."

I went to the lot and found my car with all the windows shot out and blood everywhere inside. This was my grandmother's car that I had bought a few months after she passed away. The car had been in mint condition; now it was completely destroyed.

In the past, I would deal with heartbreak by trying to be funny. So, I got some friends to make a video of thugs stealing my vehicle. I had the song, "I'm too fly for a white guy," where I was drunk and acting like a gangster. In the video, I was giving a Colt 22 beer to my best friend's kid. Of course, I didn't give him any alcohol; we were just acting silly. After posting this video, it quickly went viral. Fans were calling me a racist and stating that I gave alcohol to a minor. I pulled it off Facebook, but it was too late, as my enemies had saved the video and started sharing it on the Chiefs fan pages.

I developed a "Don't give a crap about what others think about me" attitude. It cut deep when I saw people who I thought were close friends trashing my name on social media. Why were they silent when I did amazing things for others in the past and now, when I was struggling, they didn't reach out to help me? Instead, they were throwing out my struggles for the world to see and talking behind my back. I was confused about who my true friends were. Having such a big circle by being "famous" made it difficult to know who I could trust.

In the next few months, everything I did on social media was questioned, and I made the mistake of making videos expressing my feelings when I was drunk. This made negative things spread like wildfire. I realized how famous the XFactor image had become because even though training camp was approaching, I had become the hot topic in the Chiefs Kingdom. I gave ammunition to all my haters, and their lies became truth to many. If I was drinking and acting crazy, then lies being spread must be true. I really didn't care what others said or thought about me. I was lost in pride and didn't care about anything anymore.

With that attitude, I went off the deep end with chemical use and surrounded myself with those who wanted to party and get the perks of hanging with XFactor. People treated me differently because I was XFactor, and some enabled me because of who I was. People would give me free drinks and drugs so they could hang with me.

This lifestyle also brought women. I started dating 19 and 20-year-old strippers. This brought on the criticism that I was a dirty old man taking advantage of young girls. I would ask, "Why can others do the exact same thing I'm doing and not suffer the same consequences?" The devil consumed my life with pride, greed, and lust.

Resentments and pain came with this lifestyle. My loved ones distanced themselves because they couldn't stand the pain of watching me die in front of their eyes. My new friends were fake and wanted to use me to satisfy their own desires. I felt alone and my chemical use became worse to escape it.

My phone constantly vibrated with, "Did you see what so and so posted about you on social media?" I had to defend my image, and I tried to keep others out of the drama. For the first time, I started saying, "I don't want to be XFactor anymore. I want to be a person no one knows and not a person that everyone is talking about." The life I had worked to build was crashing down all around me and I didn't care.

Then, something started happening as many people were praying for me. The devil had such a grip on me, but looking back, God was showing me grace and mercy. I had some scary situations where death was knocking on my door, but I wasn't scared because death would end the insanity. God would inject guardian angels into my life to protect me from harm. I couldn't understand how complete strangers would appear and help me through a tough situation and then quickly disappear. I also had loved ones who wouldn't give up on me even though I had given up on myself.

My mom came to save her son and found me alone talking to my angels in Heaven. She asked me to go to rehab again, which I agreed to, as I was completely and totally broken. On the long drive, she realized what I was dealing with as my phone never stopped vibrating with text messages. At one point, it had driven her so crazy that she threatened to throw it out the window. She saw firsthand that I couldn't escape the insanity that was going on with social media.

Upon checking into the treatment facility, everyone treated me differently because I was "famous." On the third night, I decided to walk to the store to get smokes without permission. I was struggling to follow the rules. The next day, my counselor informed me that they were going to kick me out of treatment. She asked the patient group if they wanted me to stay or go. Everyone went on my behalf to ask the management if I could get another chance, but their minds were made up. I was told that if I returned, I would be arrested for trespassing. I went to a motel across the street and when I got into a room, I immediately started drinking again.

I was arrested one night for trespassing because I left gifts for treatment center friends on the curb by the road. I hadn't stepped one foot on the property, but I spent that night in jail. The next morning after bonding out, I decided to make a Facebook live video. I said, "There are two footprints in the sand. I'm here but these aren't my footprints. They are God's and He is carrying me because I don't have strength to walk on my own." I closed the video by saying, "I'm coming home." I meant that I was going to find a ride to my hometown, but everyone on social media thought I was going to kill myself and go to God.

Immediately, my friends and family who saw the video called 911 in Norton, Kansas. A police officer came and said, "We have to stop this craziness. We received around 1000 phone calls about you planning to kill yourself." I agreed to go with him to the station, and my mom asked them to do a mental evaluation. I agreed to this and the doctor recommended that I go to a state hospital.

Before I left, a fax came into the police station saying that my ex had filed a restraining order against her and my daughter. I never received this order from the police as they were consumed with where they were going to take me. On the way to Larned State Hospital, God started showing me signs. I could predict songs that were on other stations. Kansas City started to extradite me to the state hospital closer to KC. They had filed charges against me for getting into a fight with 7 bikers at a bar a month earlier. This made the police officer driving extremely mad and he kept saying, "He is under my custody and I'm not driving him all the way to KC."

God put on my heart that a miracle would happen in 9 minutes at 9:11 p.m. I told the other deputy that a miracle would happen at 9:11. I even counted down the last 10 seconds till the clock on the radio turned to 9:11. The officer was on the phone screaming to his supervisor about the situation and all his frustrations. As soon I hit zero in counting down, the officer asked his supervisor, "What? Are you serious?" He hung up the phone and told the deputy, "I can't believe that just happened. All of a sudden, KC went from demanding that we bring Ty to them to saying just go ahead and take him to Larned."

The other deputy said, "Ty counted down and said a miracle would happen at that exact moment." The officer had a puzzling look on his face, as I had been telling him what songs were on other radio stations. And now this. He said, "I can't deal with anymore of this craziness, Ty. Please go to sleep." Upon arriving at the state hospital, I realized I was crossing off the second X they talked about in AA.

1. Jail
2. Institution
3. Death.

For many years I had worked for an adult handicapped facility nearby and had brought many of my individuals suffering from behavior issues to this state hospital. Now I was on the other side of the fence for the first time in my life. In the past, my clients would get worse in state hospitals as they would drug them on new meds. Immediately, they ordered medication to put me on. I was needing treatment, not different mind-altering chemicals.

I was hungry and asked for some crackers and grape juice that the nurses had in the break room. A girl asked, "How did you get crackers and grape juice?" I shared them with her and asked her name, which she said Mary. This was the first sign from God, and I thought about Jesus breaking bread and sharing wine with His disciples, plus the name of Jesus' mom was Mary.

After my snack, I walked around the ward and the name tags on their rooms were Bible names. Peter, John, Paul, James, etc. I went to my room and looked outside the window. I saw visions of the most horrible destruction which were followed by visions of the most beautiful things. My pastor later told me these were visions of the life God was giving me. Either I could continue on the road with the devil, and it would bring devastation on my loved ones, or I could follow God and receive all His blessings.

A man interrupted this and asked, "Hi. I'm Nathaniel. Would you like to walk with me?" I learned that he was fellow addict, now his life was a complete mess due to pharmaceutical drugs they kept prescribing him. He was very smart and consumed with addictions like me. As a matter of fact, he was released the day I left.

Later that night, I was scared by a man who looked exactly like Kyle, the man I wrote about earlier. The only difference was that he was walking, and he said, "Hi, my name is Kyle." This really messed with my head, and I thought, "Am I about to die or is this a bad dream?"

Later that night, they gave me meds that knocked me out. The next day, Nathaniel said the drugs made me act like a zombie. I didn't recall anything he said that I had done. That's when I made the decision to reject the medications they gave me to solve my problems. I knew it would only cause new addiction problems. (I think that 90 percent of the people in the treatment center I had just left were there for prescription drugs.)

That morning, I had a meeting with my support group and my doctor. I called the doctor an "instrument of the devil, a legal drug dealer," and requested counseling, which they didn't have. I wasn't going to allow them to drug me like they did for individuals I had worked with. This had major consequences, as the judge wouldn't release me because he based his decision on the doctor's recommendations. I stayed a week before I convinced the judge to release me. At that time, I was so mad because of being locked up in a place I didn't belong, but looking back, God put me in there to protect me from outside dangers. Everything that had happened, especially all signs from God, scared me as I thought I truly was losing my mind.

Upon leaving the hospital, I returned to alcohol to escape everything. I went back to the motel in Norton to retrieve my belongings. Nathan and I decided to go to the swimming pool, and the kids thought it was awesome to have XFactor there. The police came again and asked me to leave town because my haters had posted I was a sexual predator. All of which were lies. I had given the kids autographed XFactor cards. In small town America, rumors spread like crazy. So, we left.

We headed toward my hometown and, upon arriving, were immediately pulled over. People on social media were tracking my whereabouts and rumors were spreading like wildfire. I wasn't the man people were lying about and portraying me to be. We decided to drive all night and go to KC to escape all the drama in Western Kansas.

The next day, I went to the Chiefs Training Camp with a girl I was dating. I got a call from Nathan, who stayed at my store to sleep. He said that five bikers had showed up looking for me. They had pointed guns in his face and asked, "Are you a part of Ty's Posse? If you are, we are going to shoot you." Nathan convinced them he wasn't, and then he immediately left town.

Upon arriving back at my store, my former apprentice, my ex's fiancé, and 3 other bikers showed up. They stood outside in the street taunting me, trying to get me to come off my property and to fight them. They knew I would call the cops and have them arrested for trespassing if they came onto the property. Little did I know that my old apprentice was filming me, and I made a huge mistake. After 30 minutes of taunts, I mooned them and then flashed my genitals at them. This video went viral and lies spread that I was exposing myself with kids around. (Not one kid was present.)

I called the police as soon as the bikers showed up, but it took the police 45 minutes to get there. The bikers told the cops they had a warrant out for my arrest for violating a restraining order. The paper that police in Norton, Kansas had received, which I never got, was a form saying that the restraining order had been approved. I had reached out a few days earlier to the mother of my daughter to see if I could see her. She had set me up by telling my mother that my daughter missed me, and I could see her when I got back to KC. I had no clue she had filed this restraining order so by texting her she went to the police and showed proof I had violated a restraining order.

I was handcuffed and taken to jail. This was on July 30th, 2017, and was held on $500 bond. When arrested, I didn't have my wallet or my phone, so the only numbers I knew by heart were to my family. They made the decision to not bond me out because they thought jail was the safest place for me. Which was crazy to me because I was in jail with murderers. My family had heard rumors of others threatening to kill me. Jail was a slap in my face, but I needed it to say I got to end this journey of self-destruction. I had lost everything in my life, including hope.

On the fifth day, I hit my knees and asked God for a glimmer of hope. I asked for forgiveness for saying I didn't believe in Him. I told Him that He was the only One who could save me from myself. I read the Bible the last 5 days I was in jail and I started process of surrendering. That's when I decided to quit the devil's number 1 poison that he used to control me: drugs and alcohol. The devil knows that it is the XFactor that can completely destroy me.

I would not wish this storm on anyone! That being said, I'm beyond thankful and grateful that I went through this storm because it led me back to Jesus and God. It taught me valuable lessons. It humbled me, as I was a man consumed with pride. It taught me how greed, lust, resentments, and anger could destroy me. It showed me who the negative and positive XFactor's in my life were. I found out who loved me so much that they would fight for me and be with me during my hard times. I learned who was in my life to use me to satisfy their wants and needs, those who would turn into an enemy as soon as things got rough.

In my storm, I thought I was only hurting myself. But I learned how much it hurt everyone involved. Being so close to my grave, I appreciate and am beyond grateful for God's mercy to keep me here. I learned that, even though I had quit God, He never gave up on me. God fought for my soul because He still had a greater purpose while I'm blessed to be on Earth.

God revealed Himself to me again at church, the day after I got out of jail. I went to the altar and a pastor told me, "God put on my heart that they were not your angels, but they were His, and they are with Him."

The next 6 months were a struggle as I dealt with the consequences of my actions. With God's help, nothing was as much a struggle as when I was going through spiritual warfare. I've been to the darkest places that few come back from. A place where only God could have saved me. By reliving the toughest times of my life, it can be XFactor to help those struggling where I once did. To pray forward what has been given to me. Some will forever hold my past against me, but God doesn't and that's all that matters to me.

Hopefully it will open the eyes of others on how they can be an XFactor by sharing God's Word. Will you be a light to them or will you bring darkness into their world? In the darkest storms, you will find out which side of the fence your friends are on. Don't let the devil distract you with actions or words of others. Listen to people who have God in their lives who only want what is best for you. Use haters as motivation to become a better person, living more like Jesus did.

I look to positive XFactor's in my life to inspire me to be as loving as they are. Through the death of my angels, I now see that He placed them in my life to teach me and to have my faith grow in Him. Even in death some are chosen to inspire us to change our ways. The brightest candles burn out the quickest. We all have a purpose on Earth. Blessed are the ones who discover their purpose is to help build up others.

All my life the devil deceived me by saying, "You do amazing things for kids, so you can be a bad boy once in a while." I would go to the gentleman's clubs and tell friends that it was adult charity work supporting single mothers and college funds a dollar at a time. I dated girls who worked at these clubs because they didn't get jealous of the attention I got. This is part of what spiritual warfare is when you sin in so many areas inviting the devil and demons into your soul.

The Holy Spirit, Jesus and God will fight for you, but you can't just keep letting evil in. My spiritual warfare was just getting started, and it really got crazy once I started to try to turn my life over to God but still have the devil orchestrating many things.

"Finally, be strong in the Lord and in his mighty power.
Put on the full armor of God, so that you can take your stand
against the devil's schemes."
Ephesians 6:10-11

"But the Lord is faithful, and he will strengthen you
and protect you from the evil one."
2 Thessalonians 3:3

CHAPTER 26

Spiritual Warfare #2

In 2019, spiritual warfare arose when I lost three angels in a month. I was struggling with selling vehicles, as it's not a very godly career. With pressures of football coming, many opportunities arose. I was struggling internally as the devil was tempting me in many ways.

One day after Shon's funeral, I decided to quit my job and focus on building my t-shirt business. At this point, so many people attacked me about my past on social media. The devil was deceiving me by saying I could go to bad environments again, especially strip clubs. Everything was dividing me from my relationship I had been building with God. Internally a war began for my soul as I was inviting evil back in. God started showing me signs that He was present in my life, but the devil went on a full blown attack.

With everything going on, it became too much to handle. My actions and words seemed like I had relapsed, but the truth was I just couldn't handle everything. I was being pulled in a million directions and distracted by all my haters. I had saved a lot of money from being a successful car salesman. To cope with stress in my life, I started spending money like crazy, buying things for others as that brought me happiness.

When I told others that I was going through spiritual warfare, they didn't believe me and accused me of relapsing. My mom came to town to take me to treatment again, which was last place I needed to go. I hadn't had a drop of any chemical. When she arrived, I was hiding in a motel as I was being attacked even by strangers. That's how the devil works in using others to do his evil deeds.

I got into a heated argument with my mom, which rarely happened in past. All of a sudden, God placed in my heart to run. I took off on foot trying to find a place where I could be alone with God and battle the devil. I found a stream and knew water would throw off police if they were called to find me. I made the decision to make a video where I was washing money that I thought was dirty money from selling vehicles. This caused people to worry about me and was used as proof to critics that I had relapsed. I didn't need help from any person, but I needed Jesus to help me, as the devil was attacking my mind and heart.

Being in nature was the best thing and is always where I go when I need a break from life. I shut my phone off and walked farther and farther away from civilization. It was beyond hot outside and, luckily, I found some woods that were cooler. I sat down and began to pray. God put a peace in my heart being with him away from all the craziness. I stood up to continue walking and felt a pain go through my right foot. I looked down and a nail was coming out the top of my shoe. I pulled my foot off the nail and fell to the ground. I pulled off my bloody sock and saw my foot bleeding from both sides. I washed it off in creek and put my wet money around the injury, tying the money on with a pink ribbon I had found earlier. I cleared the overgrowth around me and realized I had been praying on an old homestead. I found a walking stick and started walking again.

It amazed me as, with each step, it felt like God was healing my foot. After a few miles, I cast away my walking stick and began to walk normally. After walking around a cornfield, I was confronted by two ladies on a four wheeler. I had set off their game cameras, and they told me I was trespassing. I apologized and said I was just walking in nature.

A few miles down the road, I found a horse ranch that gave rides to kids. I was grateful to be able to buy some water, as I was dehydrated. A few miles later, I arrived in the town of Greenwood. I was scared by my best friend, Rob, who came running up next to me. He had started tracking me because everyone was afraid. Being a small town farm boy that had hunted, he had followed clues and talked to people who had seen me. I said, "Run with me." After a few blocks, he said, "I need to get my vehicle so we can go home." I lost him by doubling back on side streets. Last thing I wanted was to go back to the chaos that was going on in my life in KC.

I found a convenience store so I could get food and water. Right behind it were some trees and bushes. I decided to hide there and prayed for the next few hours. After a little while, a lot of motorcycles appeared in town. Rob had put on social media I was last seen in Greenwood heading east.

The previous few weeks, I had been getting threats from one of my biggest haters who belonged to a local biker organization. They were coordinating a search for me at the gas station, about 100 feet from me, and I heard their conversations on where I might be heading. I used brush to camouflage myself. As dark ascended, I could see lightening approaching. This was a sign of a storm raging in my soul. I glanced at social media on my phone and bit was beyond crazy. People were saying I was armed because I had said on the video that God had armed me. I was talking about being armed with the Bible.

When the storm got close, I could see three bikers sneaking around the back of the gas station. I know they suspected I was hiding in the trees, but they didn't come back there because they thought I had a gun. Eventually a thunderstorm came and God poured rain on me. The rain brought peace as bikers had left before it had gotten there. I finally got on social media, and a friend gave me a ride home.

Early that next morning, I was awakened by two police officers knocking on my bedroom door. Someone had called them saying I was suicidal. After about 15 minutes, I convinced them I wasn't suicidal and they left. I spent that day looking at social media and discovered the wolves had come out casting all kinds of lies about me. By responding to negativity, it only made things worse.

That night coming home from the store, a tornado warning came over the radio, and God put on my heart another attack was coming. I rushed home and decided to hide in the woods behind my house. I had a fire pit behind my house and, a few days earlier, I had made a cross with two logs. Walking toward my fire pit, I could see that there was a fire in it, and that cross was on fire. This scared me to my core, as I sensed something bad was coming in my direction. I put the fire out with water and went into the woods with my Bible.

I heard bikes around my house and neighborhood. Then I saw people walking around my house and the backyard with flashlights. I heard lightening in the background, and after a while, all the bikes fired up and left. I continued to pray until rain started coming down on me. I realized that God was using thunderstorms as a sign that danger was approaching. There was ultimate storm going on for my soul.

I started receiving scary phone calls and threats from private numbers. At 4 a.m., I called my good friend, Josh, who I had sold vehicles with. He asked if I could meet him at church and when I arrived, Josh was waiting. I told him all the crazy things that had been going on and how scared I was. Josh kept saying, "Help is on the way." A pickup driving by a man named David pulled up. (David was a man I had sold vehicles with for a few months." I didn't know that David was also the pastor for this church. I started pouring everything out to David and Josh.

The rain moved in, so David opened the church for us to enter. After about an hour of me telling all that was happening, David said, "Ty, you are going through what is called spiritual warfare. There is a tremendous storm raging inside you because you have a huge platform that the devil wants because you can influence so many people. By you trying to seek God on your own, this is making the devil up his game in trying to destroy you."

David's words made a light go off in my heart. What everyone else thought was me using drugs, David had given me a name for it and explained it. David said, "I believe you that you haven't relapsed, amd that it takes on that appearance. You aren't handling this storm very well because you are trying to control it. God is calling for you, and you need to completely turn your life over to him."

I answered, "I will start coming to this church." I had been struggling to find a church because every pastor would glorify me by saying, "Isn't it so amazing that XFactor is here! He will bring many others to our church." This church was different and I could feel the presence of the Holy Spirit. I somewhat understood what was happening and knew a direction for healing.

The next few months, the devil continued to attack. But at church, I learned how to pray against evil. I was like a young kid at school, eager to learn about God and Jesus. Through this horrible storm, I learned about God's mercy and grace. He had been saving me from things I deserved (mercy) and blessing me with things I didn't (grace).

"The weapons we fight with are not the weapons of the world. On the contrary, they have divine power to demolish strongholds. We demolish arguments and every pretension that sets itself up against the knowledge of God, and we take captive every thought to make it obedient to Christ."
2 Corinthians 10:4-5

"Be alert and of sober mind. Your enemy the devil prowls around like a roaring lion looking for someone to devour. Resist him, standing firm in the faith, because you know that the family of believers throughout the world is undergoing the same kind of sufferings."
1 Peter 5:8-9

CHAPTER 27

Spiritual Warfare #3

The devil starts a full attack right after loved ones pass away.

In 2021, I lost three close friends and the onslaught began again. The devil knows how much my heart loves, so he attacks when I'm at my weakest. Once again, attacks about my past started on the internet. I took another job in sales, as it is a way I can make easy money. The devil knows this and throws stress at me through work.

I was doing a Facebook live video after I got out of shower. I thought the video had stopped and reached for my secondary phone when it rang. A few minutes later, I started getting messages that my genitalia were on the video. I went in and removed the video, but the damage was done as someone had recorded it and later passed it on to my biggest hater.

Once again, I started trending negatively on social media, and my roommate started flipping out on me. The mother of my child even tried to lie to courts again and get restraining orders against me for her and my daughter.

When something like this happens, people always get my family and loved ones involved by messaging them and asking what's wrong with me.

When I went to the state hospital in 2017, I was diagnosed as bipolar and manic. At the time, I was under the influence of alcohol and drugs, so I felt this wasn't the issue. I would be normal most of the time, except when I went through spiritual warfare. When this happened, I wouldn't remember things I said to others, and I would send hurtful pictures or say mean things to those I loved. It was like my brain would become so stigmatized from all the attacks coming that I would go blank. Everyone said, "It's your bi-polar and manic. You need to get on medications to control it." I tried to explain that I didn't think that's what was going on.

My spiritual warfare episodes had gotten shorter in length but with stronger intensity. I couldn't understand why I was being attacked more when my life was all about God. I was learning to turn to God faster and surrendering. I went to a Wednesday Bible Study at my church and God was speaking directly to my heart. The previous Sunday, the pastor said that I should ask God to search my heart. He warned me that it was scary, but boy, I had no clue what I was inviting.

After Bible Study was over, I was praying at my chair when I lost all control of my body and collapsed to the floor. My pastor and his wife found me lying face down when they were cleaning up the chapel. The pastor's wife said, "Honey, do you smell smoke radiating from Ty?" As he shook me, he replied, "Yes, it smells like sulfur from hell." My body was paralyzed and I couldn't respond back. My pastor realized what was happening, called the elders from the church and other pastors from other churches. Soon everyone was there praying over me and saying, "Ty, just say Jesus."

I had no control of my body and was the most frightened I had ever been. Many people tried to roll me over so I could look them in face, but they said I had unbelievable strength. They said I would crawl across the floor like a snake trying to get away from their prayers. All I remember is clutching onto my Bible and my necklace crosses, praying inside my head for God to make it all stop. On three occasions, my body would start shaking like I was having a seizure. I would have the worst pain imaginable on the inside and then I would throw up. My pastor would scream, "Yes, Ty, get that out of you."

Finally, after four and half hours of praying over me, I was able to repeat back "Jenna," my daughter's name. Then I was able to say "Jesus, Jesus, Jesus." I started getting control of my body and began to cry uncontrollably.

Later on, my pastor said that I had vomited out three demons. He also said, "I have helped many with demonic possessions, but never had the devil not looked me in the face." In all that time, not once were they able to get me to look at them in the face. This was the scariest thing I've ever experienced, but that is when true change started happening.

After this incident, I met my brother Josh. He said that the night he met me at the church at 4 a.m., it was the scariest thing he had seen, and he thought I was going to kill him. He said my beautiful blue eyes were solid black, and the things I was saying wasn't me talking.

About a month after this happened, I was asked to go to the movies by one of my best friends. I let her pick the movie, and she picked "Conjuring 2." She loved scary movies, so I said, "That is fine." The movie scared me but not like other people in attendance. The movie was about demonic possession and how the demons take over people's bodies completely. It was based on a true story where a young man killed people after getting possessed. It was like my story was being played on the big screen. Like I said, when I would be in spiritual warfare I would do or say horrible things and not have any memory of it.

I'm sure I picked up those three demons during my years of chemical abuse. I finally understood why even though I was seeking God more and more every day, the attacks were happening inside my head. Every day now I can feel the Holy Spirit working inside me. Sure, I struggle with sin, but I don't have evil inside me anymore. I feel like a brand-new creation and the most unbelievable peace is in my soul, even when storms arise.

This experience also helped me to be compassionate to anyone who hates me, my enemies. I understand that they could have spirits controlling their words and actions. I can forgive and pray against evil in their lives. To truly love and have compassion for them.

The most difficult one to love and forgive was myself. I realized that no matter what has happened, God and Jesus always loved me more than I can comprehend. Who am I not to forgive myself and love how God made me? The three times I went through spiritual warfare were the scariest times of my life. Through them, though, is how my unquestioned faith arose and all my chains were broken from the devil. At many points I would say, "I can't do this," and try to run. But there's no escaping what's inside you. I had to find out how to fight through my Savior.

I never want to go through battles like I have the last four years since surrendering. The blessing now is that I can be that steadfast friend to anyone who is going through this. Maybe my story can open the eyes to ones being misdiagnosed and who are sinking deeper and deeper. I'm a firm believer that we are surrounded by angels and demons. So much peace comes from knowing that God will send angel armies to protect me and I have the Holy Spirit to guide my journey. I pray every day that God grows and prunes me. I also pray that He gives me opportunities to help lead others to His saving light!

"Submit yourselves, then, to God. Resist the devil,
and he will flee from you."
James 4:7

"No, in all these things we are more than conquerors through him who loved us. For I am convinced that neither death nor life, neither angels

*nor demons,[a] neither the present nor the future, nor any powers,
neither height nor depth, nor anything else in all creation, will be able
to separate us from the love of God that is in Christ Jesus our Lord."*
Romans 8:37-39

*"The thief comes only to steal and kill and destroy;
I have come that they may have life, and have it to the full."*
John 10:10

*"I [Jesus] have told you these things, so that in me you may have peace.
In this world you will have trouble. But take
heart! I have overcome the world."*
John 16:33

*"No temptation has overtaken you except what is common to
mankind. And God is faithful; he will not let you be tempted
beyond what you can bear. But when you are tempted, he
will also provide a way out so that you can endure it."*
1 Corinthians 10:13

CHAPTER 28

Banned From Arrowhead

In October of 2021, I relapsed after being clean and sober for 4 years. I fell right back into drinking and cocaine use like I had never quit. I was half business owner of a carpet cleaning business. Very shortly after my relapse, my co-owner got into a huge fight that ended with me going to jail for trespassing at his house. My roommate and I also got into a fight when we were both drunk. I found myself without a job and homeless. This sent me in a downward spiral, as I had all the time and money in the world to get completely messed up all day long.

I was living at the lake in my vehicle and fishing every day. There was an enormous game against the Buffalo Bills coming up on Sunday Night Football. That morning, I woke up and immediately started drinking. I had lost almost everything again and didn't care anymore. I had gone to the Chiefs games for the previous 10 years completely sober every time. Today would be different as I didn't care anymore about anything, except my image.

My best friend Don "Chiefs Santa" came to the lake to take me to the game. Since I was already drunk, he drove me to Arrowhead Stadium. At the stadium, I always got there extremely early, which was the case once again. Typically, we would walk around in every parking lot, firing up the fans. Being drunk, I didn't want to do this for the first time in 10 years. I decided to go to a friend's tailgate that had free beer, as my supply was running low. That whole tailgating experience is still a blur, as I partied just like so many thousands of other Chiefs fans. I always was in my seat inside the stadium an hour before kickoff, but this night I must have arrived after kickoff. What happened next, I have no recollection.

Somehow, I ended up in the wrong section and underhanded a bottle of water at my biggest enemy. A video shot by a fan that would later go viral shows Tim "RedXtreme" running up the stairs at me. I grabbed his jersey, he confronts me, and he then knocks me out with a right punch. I went tumbling down the stairs. The next thing I remember is being in triage getting looked over. It took a couple of law enforcement officers to help me up the stairs to triage, as I was told later.

After being examined, they escorted me out of the stadium. It was raining, but somehow, I found a bus to get out of elements since Don had the keys to my vehicle. After the game, the bus owner found me and called for an ambulance. Luckily Don found me before I left in the ambulance and followed me to the hospital. I found out I had 4 broken ribs from falling down the stairs. After being discharged, we got a motel room. The next morning, my phone blew up with news reporters wanting to interview me on what had happened. So, in my hospital gown, I did a few interviews.

On Twitter, the video had millions of hits, so that led to more interviews. I was on local news stations, then TMZ, and the Pat McAffee show, to name a few. RedXtreme and I had gone back many years with him trying to fight me. At one point, He was my best friend. I had helped him become a Superfan and even given him the name. I had taken him to Hawaii for the Pro Bowl for setting the Guiness World Record after watching 70 straight hours of football. He repaid me by sleeping with the mother of my child.

After this happened, I took away his tickets next to me, kicked him out of my charity organization, KCSuperfans, and no longer called him friend. For years he would tell charity organizations, my jobs, and friends lies about me. He said I was a pedophile, stole from charities, was a meth addict, etc. I was told by a friend that right before I threw the bottle of water, RedXtreme had been standing on his seat trying to get the crowd louder. When he used to sit next to me, this behavior always made me mad, as people behind him couldn't see the game. That's no excuse for my actions and, if I had been sober, the whole incident wouldn't have happened.

The next week sucked as I was in so much pain from four broken ribs. I drank as much as I could and ate edibles of marijuana to be able to function. I had tickets to the Chiefs verses Washington Football team in Washington the very next weekend. My best friend Rob had tons of free flyer miles, motel, and rental car points so I would buy tickets to away games, and he would supply everything else.

That Friday as we were getting ready to fly out, I received an email from the Chiefs. It stated that I was banned from all Chiefs functions including games at Arrowhead, training camp, draft, etc. I was in shock that this was happening, but I was drunk, so it didn't set in. I was hurt that the email came from Jayne who I had worked with on the Guiness World Records for crowd noise. I thought my relationship with the Chiefs was good. Why had I not been called and interviewed by them?

I also learned that RedXtreme only got a 1-year ban and mine was a lifetime ban. Supposedly this was my second offense. In 2017, RedXtreme filed a complaint that I was charging for photos and handing out business cards promoting my business endeavors. I met with the Chiefs and thought this had been proven as lies.

Going to Washington was a distraction and I thought I would deal with the ban when I got back to Kansas City. My trip to Washington was a blur, as I was drunk all waking hours. I had thousands of fans say,

"I saw you on TMZ" or "I saw you on the Pat McAfee show." Everyone was throwing alcohol my way in exchange for photos with me. The ban ended my streak of 344 straight games at Arrowhead Stadium, and I haven't gone to another away game since. I now watch all the games on TV.

There are times that I miss my old life as a Superfan but being in the spotlight no longer has its advantages. I will eventually start going back to away games as I've been to 106 over the years, including a Super Bowl in Miami. Alcohol and drugs have cost me so much in my lifetime. Losing my kids and XFactor are the two toughest pills to shallow.

Alcohol and drugs don't discriminate; they just cause destruction.

CHAPTER 29

Bipolar/Manic

In 2017 I was diagnosed with bi-polar and being manic, which go along with me being an alcoholic and addict. Here are the symptoms I experience every time I have a manic episode.

- Energy: Feeling full of energy, more active than usual, or restless
- Speech: Talking a lot, speaking very quickly, or not making sense to others
- Sleep: Decreased need for sleep, sleeping very little or not at all, or waking up early
- Thoughts: Uncontrollable racing thoughts, quickly changing ideas or topics when speaking, or disturbed or illogical thinking
- Distractibility: Being easily distracted or having poor concentration
- Impulsivity: Increased risky or impulsive behavior, such as reckless driving, spending sprees, or sexual promiscuity
- Mood: Feeling very happy, elated, or overjoyed, or feeling incredibly "high" or euphoric

- Self-importance: Delusions of self-importance or feeling extremely self-confident and unrealistic about abilities (grandiosity)
- Other: Dressing more colorfully, being less inhibited, having inappropriate sexual activity, or making poor choices in spending or business

Every time I have a manic episode, I lose my belongings, spend thousands of dollars, and end up incarcerated.

My episodes can also lead to me relapsing to cope with symptoms. I begin by giving all my belongings away and spending lots of money buying gifts for friends and family. It has also cost me many jobs as I go crazy with business ideas and spend lots of money trying to make them become a reality.

I currently go to a therapist and take medication to stabilize me, so I don't go into manic episodes. So many that follow me blame my issues on alcohol, drugs, or being XFactor, but many of my problems stem directly to my bi-polar and manic episodes.

My irrational behavior looks like a relapse to everyone looking in from the outside. I have learned so much about my disorders that with therapy, diet, medications, etc., they are currently under control.

CHAPTER 30

The Reason

My mom always said that God saved me and kept me on Earth for a reason. I've seen so many friends die from addiction, in car crashes, suicide, etc. Looking back, I realize that it was God who saved me from overdosing, from killing myself in a car wreck, or spared my life in those crazy times I said, "Hold my beer and watch this."

Fans are shocked when they learn I've been to Oakland Coliseum four times as XFactor and lived to talk about it. But that was less scary than those moments behind the scenes where I should have died.

God saved me twice from sinking a boat and not drowning. The last time was in 36-degree water which I could have died from hypothermia after being in water for 45 minutes. The devil will attack me trying to steal from me, kill me, and destroy me because he knows how many people I can influence.

In a similar way, God always tried to have a relationship with me. Even when I was lost in the wilderness for so many years, God was with me, even though I didn't know He was. I've had more second chances than I'll ever know. I am fortunate to still be here, as so many don't get another chance.

The reason I'm writing this book and sharing my testimony is in the hope that it touches one life and saves that life. Maybe that person is you, or maybe it's one of your loved ones who is struggling. I hope that it can inspire one person to take a different road than what I did, one of less danger and heartache.

If this book can one life, then it is worth the countless hours it took to write it. How different my world would be if I had died. I have done many things I'm not proud of, but I have also done amazing things that have impacted many lives. I know God has kept me around so I can be a positive XFactor to everyone I come in contact with, and through social media - some I will never meet.

My purpose in life is to glorify God in all my actions. This book is a part of that. Without God keeping me alive, I would not be able to write this for you.

"But I have raised you up for this very purpose,
that I might show you my power and that my name
might be proclaimed in all the earth."
Exodus 9:16

"And we know that in all things God works
for the good of those who love him,
who have been called according to his purpose."
Romans 8:28

CHAPTER 31

Guardian Angels

Everyone we meet has an impact on our lives.

Throughout my life, I have had many family, friends, and angels grow their angel wings and leave way too soon. I keep them in my heart and use what they taught me to help myself and others.

For a long time, my question and doubt about God had me struggling when death happened. Through experiences and signs, my emotions have moved from hurt and pain to faith. I know there is an amazing life after death, moreso than I can imagine. Death no longer scares me; because I know that Heaven awaits us if we simply believe in Jesus. I tell people that the day I die will be the greatest day of my life because I will be promoted that day for eternity.

I'm fortunate to be able to speak to others about my faith who are grieving the loss of their loved ones. Our legacy is left in the seeds we planted in others while we are on Earth. But I don't want a legacy; I want them to know Jesus. So many people inspire us and touch our lives; that's the most important thing they can leave behind.

Someday when God calls me home, it will be a glorious day, as I'll get to see everyone who impacted my life. I talk daily to my guardian angels who are in Heaven. I ask them for guidance, protection, and signs to help me choose the right paths. When going through the darkest times of my life, I could always sense my guardian angels protecting me. Many times, they would give me signs about dangers ahead of me. I didn't recognize those signs quickly enough and I crashed and burned. Now, I feel their presence with me, which brings peace to my heart.

At every Chiefs game, I turn to where the flag is flying above the stadium. God puts flashes/visions of each of my angels in my head. I can feel strength come into my body when this happens and that strength gets me ready to give all I have at Arrowhead.

Many times, our guardian angels appear as complete strangers. They help us through a tough time and then disappear. It blows me away when God speaks to us through others, giving them the exact words we need to hear about what we're struggling with. Just like the Bible says, God will send His angels to watch over us. I feel beyond blessed because I know that I have so many watching over me.

> *"For he will command his angels concerning*
> *you to guard you in all ways."*
> Psalm 91:11

CHAPTER 32

Jesus and God

As a kid, my mom made me go to church, which I didn't like because I thought people were judging me and others. I was filled with doubt and questions about things I heard from Bible. This only worsened as I got older, but I still believed in God.

During my many years of addiction, I would do foxhole prayers. They would be, "God, please get me out of this, I promise I won't do it again." My prayers grew into "God, please take me tonight in my sleep as I can't endure another day on Earth."

In 2012, while in treatment, my walk with God desired a stronger relationship, but I lacked knowledge of His Word. I was consumed with questions which were doubtful. In 2017 after I relapsed and went through the horrible storm, I prayed to God for hope. That's when my journey began. This in when my eyes were opened and questions started to be answered.

After getting out of jail, I was invited to One Way Church by Shon's family. I knew the church well, as I had given my testimony there a year before. The pastor had used me as an example of people being a fan of God versus a Superfan of God. When I spoke at church, I was a fan of God; but a year later, completely broken, I started the journey of being a Superfan of God. When I did the altar call, the pastor said God had placed on his heart a message for me. "They were not my angels. They were His." That's when I went from believing there was a God to knowing there is God. That's a life altering change.

For the next year, I did a lot of growing as words from the Bible began to impact my life. For the first time, I sensed God speaking directly to my broken heart. I would go to church every Sunday, but I hadn't learned how to incorporate God into my life on other days. During this time, I was baptized, which was a special day as my mom and many loved ones made trips to see this. The pastor had me make an X with my arms when I was baptized. This was a totally different meaning to me, as it was glorifying God and not XFactor, like I had done thousands upon thousands of times in my life. It was a blessing to carry my angel Shon to be baptized right after me.

I was heartbroken when that church closed due to lack of money, and the closure is when my growth with God slowed down. I realized just how much help I needed from a pastor to learn the Word and grow from it. I bounced from church to church but couldn't find one that helped me until, through spiritual warfare, God lead me to my current church. That church is named Living Waters, which is exactly what I needed flowing through me. I started attending Bible study and services a couple of times a week. I was taught how to pray, which was new to me.

Slowly, by learning more about the Bible, I was able to start putting it into my life outside of church. I discovered that for years I thought the devil only attacked me through chemicals, which led to temptation and bad relationships, etc. What I learned was that my chemical use was just a symptom of all the underlining ways the devil would attack me. The devil attacked through pride, lust, insecurities, fear, envy, greed, doubt and worry. Through God's word, I started to learn how to put on his armor against these attacks. I learned how to lay my sins at the altar and ask for forgiveness. I would ask Jesus, through his grace and mercy, to rain down His blood over me so that my sins would be washed away. I started praying first thing in the morning and then right before I fell asleep at night. I listened only to Christian music instead of the garbage I had always listened to. This started filling my day with God, and the words in the songs spoke to my heart and filled it.

I started watching Bible movies about Jesus on TV. It was like going to school and constantly learning. But unlike my school days where I wasn't interested, I formed a fire and passion to learn everything I could. I went to work on not cussing and talking vulgar, especially about sex. I was so horrible in these areas in my past, but I had a true desire to become more Christlike.

It's amazing how God started separating me from the world so I could be alone with him. God brought me to my hometown for a few months at a time in the last year, separating me from the craziness of the big city. One of the two times I went to my hometown is when my relationship with God went to new levels. I made a commitment to read the whole Bible, from cover to cover, which took me 21 days. (I really don't like to read.)

One thing that helped me was learning that only Jesus was able to fulfill the 10 commandments and that our sins were forgiven at the cross. I never felt worthy of God's love due to all the sins in my life. Jesus's Amazing Grace washes all my past away and I get to live in His love for me.

Writing this book made it clear just how far God has changed my life from the monster I once was to the new creation He is making. God has blessed me with so many brothers and sisters in Christ to help me in my journey. It's encouraging having people constantly build me up through God's love versus having one's that bring me down. God has placed a fire in my heart to be a shepherd to those who are lost where I once was. I pray for Him to bring angels struggling with diseases or disabilities, ones suffering from addiction, depression, suicide, or whatever the devil is trying to destroy them with. I wish I could let everyone experience the peace I now have in my heart and mind. My heart, which was completely broken, is now completely filled with God's love. Everything that once was such a flaw in me is being grown into the exact opposite.

Pain is now strength, doubt is now faith, worry is now hope, pride is now humbleness, greed is now sharing, hate is now love, fear is now faith. This transformation is something I never thought would happen, but through God, it just gets better with every second of every day.

I've seen God do many miracles from saving people's lives to healing. It is amazing to scream loudly that I'm a miracle, and only God could save me from myself. To have my mind and heart healed has let me experience His amazing power. Having my soul completely consumed by darkness to now being consumed by His light that radiates in my life.

All glory goes to my Father in Heaven for doing for me what I could never do for myself. From a monster to a Child of God, this has been my journey. Every person that was an XFactor in my life, either positively or negatively, were like stars pointing me to God. It's crazy how XFactor was the biggest part of my life for 20 years, but now it led me to my number one XFactor, Jesus my Savior. Through Jesus, He will always lead me to the ultimate XFactor, our Father in Heaven!!

CHAPTER 33

New Beginnings

God saved my life by putting me in jail many times. I found God in a jail cell.

When I was in jail on two different occasions, one for six months and the other for three months, my relationship with God grew. I read the Bible three times and spent days praying and listening to Christian music. This changed my outlook on life. I went from being a completely broken man to being a healed man. I went from a monster to a Child of God. My time was spent gaining knowledge of how to have a relationship with God.

Today I spend my time going to six Bible studies each week learning from my elders how to be more Christlike. I also go to three AA and NA meetings each week, talking to newcomers about how God has removed addictions from my life. I have been 12 out of the last 13 years sober, with four relapses sprinkled in. As I'm writing this book, I have a year and half clean and sober. I haven't had a manic episode in the same amount of time. God is healing everything in my mind and body.

I've discovered a peace that I've never experienced. God has also taught me how to pray for myself and others. I spent a lot of time praying over my loved ones and have seen God do miracles in their lives. I'm embracing my new life and, where I once tried to make a name for the whole world to know, I now try to let everyone know about Jesus and what He did for us all. He died on the cross for our sins, was resurrected on the third day, then left the Holy Spirit for us. All we have to do is ask Him to be a part of our lives and to believe in Him.

I'm writing this book to help lead others to Christ, as He is the only one who can help us through our struggles. God has removed the huge circle of friends I once had and put friends in my life who truly have my best interests at heart, instead of so called friends who want something in return. I have learned how to pray for my enemies and how to forgive them for things they did to me.

I'm looking forward to what God has planned for my new life. Hopefully, this book will save at least one life. I plan to take this book into schools and give it to students who can benefit from it. I'm getting back into public speaking to tell my testimony.

I hope you have enjoyed my wild and crazy journey that God brought me through so I can share it with you. My prayers are with you and your loves ones for the struggles you encounter. God bless you all. Go Jesus, Go God, and Go Chiefs!

"For I am convinced that neither death nor life, neither angels nor demons, neither the present nor the future, nor any powers, neither height nor depth, nor anything else in all creation, will be able to separate us from the love of God that is in Christ Jesus our Lord."
Romans 8:38-39

"So we do not lose heart. Though our outer self is wasting away, our inner self is being renewed day by day. For this light momentary affliction is preparing for us an eternal weight of glory beyond all comparison, as we look not to the things that are seen but to the things that are unseen."
2 Corinthians 4:16-18

"Be strong and courageous. Do not be afraid or terrified because of them,
or the LORD your God goes with you; he will
never leave you nor forsake you."
Deuteronomy 31:6

"The LORD is my light and my salvation; whom shall I fear?
The LORD is the stronghold of my life; of whom shall I be afraid?"
Psalm 27:12

"But Jesus looked at them and said, 'With man this is impossible,
but with God all things are possible.'"
Matthew 19:26

"I can do all things through him who strengthens me."
Philippians 4:13

"Trust in the LORD with all your heart, and do
not lean on your own understanding.
In all your ways acknowledge him, and he will make straight your paths."
Proverbs 3:3-6

"'For I know the plans I have for you,' declares the LORD,
'plans to prosper you and not to harm you,
plans to give you hope and a future.'"
Jeremiah 29:11

"And we know that in all things God works
for the good of those who love him,
who have been called according to his purpose."
Romans 8:28

CHAPTER 34

New Life

It's 4 a.m. on a Sunday morning. Today is the AFC Championship game. I'm driving toward Arrowhead when my phone rings. Another one of my angels has just grown his angel's wings after a long battle with cancer. Instantly, my eyes start running like a waterfall as memories of him come rushing at me like a strong river.

I pull up to the gates at Arrowhead and fans surround my vehicle for photos. I apologize to fans for the tears in my eyes and tell them about an angel who just went to heaven. They say they will join me in prayers and thoughts for the family.

All day I tell fans from all over the world about my angel and dedicate the day to him. It always brought him so much excitement to go with me to the Chiefs games. So many memories fill my heart.

At 6 p.m., I arrive back at my XFactor SUV and see fans waiting to get pictures. We all celebrate the Chiefs going to the Super Bowl. But in my heart, I'm celebrating my angel going to the ultimate Super Bowl in Heaven.

After they leave, I hop into the driver's seat and tears flow, as I know Jesus has the wheel and that He has His wings around my angel. I reach for my Bible to read a couple of my strengthening verses. I turn on my

Pandora and Angels Amongst Us start to play. I spend time in prayer and meditation asking for strength to deal with the pain and hurt. A complete peace comes over me as I know our angel will always be with me, watching over me until the day we are reunited in Heaven.

I'm so thankful for God's grace, mercy, and love for keeping me on Earth to spread His love and word with so many. Amazingly, grace saved a wretch like me and now my soul is turning as white as snow. My experiences have lead me to the darkest places imaginable, but they make God's light even brighter. Cherish times with XFactor's in your life and try to be an XFactor that brings light into people's lives. God bless you and may God be the light on your path!!

Ty Rowton is a nationally recognized sports superfan best known as **XFactor**, as well as a speaker and advocate for faith, recovery, and hope. His journey from addiction to restoration was neither quick nor easy, but through surrendering his life to Jesus, Ty found healing and purpose. His life story reflects honesty about struggle, courage in recovery, and a deep desire to help others find renewed hope. Today, he shares his testimony to encourage others who are struggling, offering proof that even the most broken stories can be redeemed and used for good.

www.ingramcontent.com/pod-product-compliance
Lightning Source LLC
Chambersburg PA
CBHW051804050726
47598CB00006B/2420